THE GREAT
BRITISH
WRITE OFF
NO PLACE LIKE HOME

To Michael.

Phoebe Brooks

Edited by Jenni Bannister

forward**poetry**

First published in Great Britain in 2014 by:
Forward Poetry
Remus House
Coltsfoot Drive
Peterborough
PE2 9BF

Telephone: 01733 890099
Website: www.forwardpoetry.co.uk

Printed and bound in the UK by BookPrintingUK
Website: www.bookprintinguk.com

Foreword

Here at Forward Poetry our aim has always
been to provide a bridge to publication for unknown
poets and allow their work to reach a wider audience.
We believe that poetry should not be exclusive or elitist
but available to be accessed and appreciated by all.

Our latest competition **'The Great British Write Off'**
was created to celebrate the creative writing talent we
have here in the UK. We invited poets to write about a place
or area they are passionate about. The result is a collection
of verse from talented writers that, while varying in style,
expresses and communicates thoughts, feelings and ideas
about regions from across the UK to the reader. A panel
of judges will now choose their top 3 authors, who will win
either the first prize of £1450.50, the second prize of a Book
Printing voucher worth £500 or the third prize of £100.

We are proud to present this entertaining anthology
which showcases the joy and inspiration
we can all draw from where we live.

Contents

The Creative Writing

Come Gather Around

Come gather around and I'll tell you a tale
Of places and people of old
In old Weymouth town, come by wagon or sail
There is many a tale to be told.
Back when merchants set sail from the port to far lands
'Twas not only fine goods they imported
Black rats, carrying plague, crept up the wet sands
Infecting a nation that could not be thwarted.
Sir Christopher Wren, Weymouth's finest MP
Governed quarries of stone by the sheer ton
Built a cathedral so grand for the whole world to see
Named St Paul's in the city of London.
Smugglers were rife in the middle of the night
Hiding treasures, silk, satins and fine rum
But the Revenue men shot their quarry on sight
And many a smuggler was undone.
When jolly King George dipped his toes in the sea
From a bathing machine, made his entry
His followers copied with fervent glee
Fine ladies, great lords and the gentry.
The Second World War saw armadas of ships
Leave the shore for the beaches of France
They left, many knowing, 'twas a one-way trip
With nere even a backwards glance
We end our tour of ye old Weymouth town
With fine medals of silver and gold
And a space in the annals, not yet written down
The next story, so far, to unfold.

Kerry Corbin

Manchester, Wigan

What a wonderful sight it is!
When you discover the beauty of Wigan
With its enriched diversity of heritage and culture,
One can be amazed seeing River Douglas,
A wonderful gift of nature.

Many stories can be told by this great town
But only a few have come into limelight,
Why not hear what this beautiful town has to tell us
And discover its uniqueness through our sights.

What a wonderful sight it is!
When you discover that this is the home of
The Eight Lancashire Lads, a young dancing troupe,
They were the only ones who launched Charlie Chaplin's career,
Which very few people in Britain knew.

Lovingly referred to as the town of pies,
It annually holds The World Pie Eating Championship for everyone,
Bringing everyone from all walks of life together
To see who can come out as number one.

What a wonderful sight it is!
When you discover that this is the home of
Wigan Warriors, the number one rugby team in the world,
They played Australia in World Championship
And achieved recognition and praise from many countries of the world.

What a wonderful sight it is!
When you come across the Haigh Hall Manor
Built by Sir William Bradshaw in 1827-1840,
The story that this wonderful sight has to tell
Is beyond the value of any Grade 2 property.

Legend says that the ghost of Lady Mabel Bradshaw
Still haunts the manor, making it a tourist attraction,
A story that has been told for many years and years;
Which deserves many people's attention.

What a wonderful sight it is!
When you come across 'The Face of Wigan' located in Wigan town centre,
Which takes many people's breaths away,
Created by Rick Kirby the famous English sculptor
Whose artistry and creativity is still remembered today.

The town is waiting to be discovered
And it's ready with open arms to embrace you,
Discover it with open arms and hearts
And let its symphonies sway you.

Shabed Ali

Firmly Rooted

Amidst the morning's warming glow
Allows my family's tree to grow
With music, natural like a summer's breeze
When high we sway with guided ease
Where the pathways, hills and meadows lie
The shadows form and start to rise
I love this place for many reasons
The changing colours throughout the seasons
So many creatures through day and night
And I love when Mother puts things right
From people driving, riding or walking
Some deep in thought, some constantly talking
About this wonder, this natural mystery
The pathways trodden back through history
With native spawn and foreign breed
It seems Mother's duty is to always feed
And I cannot remember my very first day
When I rooted myself to the South Downs Way
As I watched Earth's canvas of artistic display
I could feel each leaf as it fell away
With ancestral rings of time on show
As I'm cut from life far down below
I was a mighty oak, I heard them say
Just one small part of the South Downs Way

C D Spooner

Look No Further

Travel the world
Explore different cultures
Experience spectacular sights
Sunset sandy beaches
Snowy mountain peaks
Look no further
Ancient Roman road
Art gallery steps
Painted places live
Victorian railway viaduct
Famous Robinson's Brewery
Hat Works Museum
Edgeley Park football
Cobbled streets walk
Hill to climb
Crowded market stalls
Once a castle
To guard where
Two rivers meet
Old police station
Now closed down
Underneath hidden away
A secret tunnel
Now a pub
World War Two
Air raid shelters
Cut deep underground
Stockport holds memories
Laughter of friends
People I know
It is somewhere
That will always
Stay so close
To my heart
Look no further
This is home.

Nigel Astell

Three Old Gentlemen Of Yorkshire

There's three old gentlemen friends of mine
Would you care to say hello?
You'll never meet such gents as these
No matter where you go.
Despite their age they never grumble
They stand proud, tall and true
And the memory of meeting them
Will last a lifetime through.
Age has not made them weary
Their bones not twisted out of place
Despite the frost of winter on their backs
And summer sun upon their faces
They live in their garden in Yorkshire
Where flowers bloom and winding streams creep
The garden is bathed with shades of green
Full of rolling hills and sheep.
So if you visit these old gentlemen
Just to tell the world you've been
Show them the respect they're due
And keep their garden clean
I'd like to introduce you
As every one of them a gent
There's Whernside, Ingleborough
And dear old Pen-y-ghent.

Glenn Rawnsley

Gateshead – North East England

My home is a house
In a street
In a town
By a river running down
To the sea.

That is me, that is mine
The North East of this land
Where the old saints once walked,
Where their steps in the sand
Took them out from their island
With a Faith and a Creed,
Where the history of England
Was written by Bede.

Between then and now
Is a long winding thread
Of a story I carry
Inside my head.
A story of love
A story of hate
Of battles and conflicts
Too long to relate.

This town we have now
So different from then,
Was built on the labour
Of poor working men.

The industrial era saw this town grow
From the sorrow and sweat of
A great human flow
Pouring in from the country
To man factory and mine,
Packed into dwellings
On the banks of the Tyne.

It has come through it all
Has this town where I live
And it stands, proud as any
With so much to give.

Part of England's North East
With its castles and forts
Countryside green
Seaside resorts
Scattered with villages
Where mining was king
Cities and towns . . .

But that's not everything

There's a house in a street
In this town, by a river
Which makes its way down to the sea

This is where I was born; this is mine

This is where I live now; this is me.

Maureen Bell

Missing Lincs

The verges plush with dandelion;
And May, banked up behind barbed wire, white as bleached bone.
This is Tennyson country:
Rape in the fields, and murder on the roads.

Though small and green yet,
Spring already has its claws into the shire,
Has drawn leaf from the raked furrows
And warmed these corners folded safe from the wind's tooth.

It was all inbreeding once, they say.
Now it's the shoots whose origins
Are dubious. A foxy lot, these squires, fed on GM crops
And robbery. The old laureate wouldn't like it.

Or would he? It's a beauty all the same:
That brook of his, those folds of land, the wolds -
Like a woman felled and pegged down,
Horizon to horizon, by church spires.

Susan Wallace

Walsall, Walsall, Walsall

The area I live
Is such a place, it makes your heart race,
At a pitt-patt of a pace.

The people rush here, there, then and now, all the while.
I went and saw the world and came back to my world.
My roots
Walsall, Walsall, Walsall,
My heart of West Midlands,
The Black Country area of the world in a dream
The living of cultures of different extremes.
An area of pure beauty,
Pure excellence,
Pure brilliance.
Walsall, Walsall, Walsall.
A town that sits all glorious,
Glamorous and wise.
In a world full of conflict.
A Constable landscape proven to paint,
A picturesque image in interesting light.
The pure potent collection of people.
From the beggars on the street,
Gathering for change
And drinking beer from cans with beggar mates.
To business people rushing by to work
With the indifference in eyes at wonderment.

Walsall, Walsall, Walsall.
Beams light to beckon you
And all to come experience
The pure joy of town at night life.
The flowing drinking punters
With fluids of beer,
Spirits and wine and good food.
The parties flowing with good cheer
And joy to be in
Walsall, Walsall, Walsall.

The old town that
Walsall, Walsall, Walsall,
Was, is still, sweet smell of leather,
Industrious wind awaking you to past times,
Now replaced with future times of changing buildings,
Changing industries and changing people.

Walsall, Walsall, Walsall.
The central post office a vital part of town,
Standing proud amongst other landmarks of
Walsall, Walsall, Walsall.
That inspired for future council dictation,
A major part of society of
Walsall, Walsall, Walsall.
You can keep London,
You can keep your Birmingham
You can keep your Wolverhampton too!
Walsall, Walsall, Walsall.
Family dos!
Cheap drink to partake,
The welcome brew in pubs all over
Walsall, Walsall, Walsall.
Town Hall civic pride,
Producing events galore that welcome you all.
The arboretum or blooming, blossoming
And creation of flowers and wildlife,
A surprising fresh air of expanding space
In time and fun for visitors.
So come on, everybody
To the single all invited individuals.
That's the *Walsall, Walsall, Walsall* experience
That makes the place.

Andrew Hinds

Beau Repaire

I know a path many have trodden before
which leads to a place born in days of yore.
Secreted away in a Prince Bishop vale -
almost certainly there is an associated tale.
It appears to be slumbering as it lies
quietly hidden under Delft blue skies.
Atmospheric mysticism all around seeping -
waiting for the darkness and mist to come creeping.
It is so quiet by day and by night,
only the stones know the story of the plight -
of the ghosts of yesteryear robbed of life -
of their joys and their sorrows, their pain and their strife.
To gaze upon it is to wonder anew,
what must have happened to the lonely few?
How many years have passed since they used to toil,
and scrape their living from this verdant soil?
There is no one now to furnish a reply -
so I am left only to muse and to sigh.
Not many go now to stand and stare -
at the lonely, ancient manor of Beau Repaire.

Lorena Owens

Hinksey Lake, South Oxford

Dawn, but the sun is reluctant to appear
and lake and mist merge.
A grebe rises, phoenix-like,
from the depths.

Catherine Bradbury

Cornwall

Cornwall is a beautiful scenic county in the west of England,
A county once known for its flourishing clay industry.
Narrow roads were busy with lorries full of clay,
Trains carried loaded clay trucks to Cornish ports each day.
Cornwall is known for many myths and legends,
Jamaica Inn, especially, for being haunted with ghostly visions.
Hidden Cornish coves and secret caves were once used for smuggling.
Boats rowed silently at night, collecting stolen goods from caves in hiding.
Cornwall has beautiful beaches and a wonderful coastline,
Panoramic views from clifftops which are breathtaking and divine,
Sparkling rivers flowing through shadowed valleys are a magnificent sight,
Forests of trees, hills, moors and green fields are a pure delight.
Cornwall has picturesque fishing villages with narrow cobbled streets,
Charming shops and friendly people, to visit is a treat.
Charlestown, Mevaggissey, Fowey and Looe and many more to see.
In summer Cornwall is packed with visitors, a lovely place to be.
There is also the Eden Project, a very popular place,
Built in a Cornish claypit with gardens, huge biomes and a rink to skate.
At Padstow there is 'Obby' Oss Day, where large crowds of people gather.
The Floral Dance is at Helston, a special day of dancing and laughter.
Bugle has the Bandsmen's Festival with brass bands coming from far and near,
Competing for the coveted awards as their proud supporters cheer.
Cornish male voice choirs from many towns and villages
Travel around the county entertaining with their perfect voices,
Sometimes singing in harmony or on the local quay,
Their loud melodious voices echoing out to sea.
Cornwall is a sporting county, with rugby and football teams,
Running and walking events to raise money for charities.
A major event is the Royal Cornwall Show each year.
Members of the Royal Family attend and hundreds of people gather.
The Hall for Cornwall is a popular place at Truro,
With a choice of professional singers, plays and shows.
From the Tamar to Land's End, with all its variety,
Cornwall is my home.

Lorna Burdon

East Ten

Outsiders call it Mattress Town
A place in decline.
There was a Bungalow Town
By the train tracks
Full of poverty, fleas and cabbages.
That was then.
We may be the same.

From the parking space
In front of number 651
Yesterday
Worldly goods
Were pushed and pulled
And first I rummaged
Hardly touching, scared of lifting
Looking for a bookshelf,
Finding curtains and rude DVDs.

A van pulled up abruptly
Urgently
And ill-dressed men
Busied themselves; pliered wires
Bent back steel and underfoot
Crushed aluminium
Watched at trolley-distance by
A Roma wife.
We smiled and connected.

Travellers came next
With hyperactive sons
And all stubbed cigarettes
On a weed-grown wall.
Oscar, shorts-clad and pony-tailed
Smelt the wood from his parish
Hostel-dwellers glimpsed
By chance.

In my street in my town
The transient residents
Come and go.
In my parish I run for buses
Protest outside buildings

Soak up rain puddles
And photograph side lines.

Whom I see are my neighbours
We talk Mandarin, and Urdu . . .
The English drop their Ts in
My town, their town
E ten Leyton.

Gillian Lawrence

Winter On The Mersey

The day is icy cold
And leaden grey
The waters of the Mersey
Uninviting, dirty, drab.
Race quickly from the scene,
Across the dismal river
Dingy warehouses and docks
Silently forlorn
Reflecting on the long forgotten glory
Of their former days
A sudden squall comes swiftly down
To hide the dreary view
Then through the swirling haze
The stately buildings on the waterfront appear
Vague misty shapes
Suggesting spectres of their wealthy past
The fussy little ferry boats
Still shuttle to and fro
But where I wonder where
Did all the big ships go.

George R Bell

Best Of British

Raise your flag, let it waft with pride,
As you decide whether your eggs should be poached or fried,
And Heinz baked beans tumble out of the tin
To pass your 'stiff upper lip' as you 'take it on the chin'.

You queue dutifully day and night,
Complain when it's dull and moan when it's too bright,
Ask about the weather, talk about it for hours,
Smile at, then sneeze at, the beautiful flowers.

Have a gossip and have a grumble
But an important complaint and you merely mumble,
As you mow the lawn of this land of contrast,
Discussing the future and reminisce of the past.

Apologies cascade . . . 'Sorry'...'I'm sorry',
Fire on and an episode of Corrie . . .
Emmerdale, Hollyoaks and EastEnders' sorrow,
We can watch those on Catch-Up tomorrow.

Get the washing on the line whilst the sun's out,
'They've forecast ten minutes!' the neighbours shout
As they lean over the fence with their garden shears
And salute this arrival with a few cold beers.

'England have qualified!' the fans will boast
And start drawing up their team over a Sunday roast,
Lashings of gravy and some Yorkshire puds,
Then washing the dishes in Fairy's suds.

'Find me a doc leaf, got stung by a nettle!'
'Bloody hell, let's put on the kettle.'
All life's problems solved over a cup of tea,
Digestive for you, Garibaldi for me.

And perhaps a plate of scones and a pot of jam
And some sandwiches with wafer thin ham,
Or a pasty or a pudding or a steak and ale pie
With garden peas, courtesy of Birds Eye.

Proper fish and chips from the chippy
And it's over five degrees, let's have a Mr Whippy,
Washed down with a pint in the local pub,
Business done and the social hub.

Love a bargain, bag a deal,
Patriotic, keep it real,
Don't be embarrassed or get all fickle . . .
Wind yourself up into a Branston pickle.

It's your country, your heritage, your roots,
So walk with pride in your sturdy Clarks boots,
Have love and respect for each and every nation,
Starting with your own – made with proud declaration.

Jackie Knowles

England

England! Oh! England, where has it gone?
The quiet peace, I used to gaze upon,
Slumbering hedgerows, drowsy bees,
Picnic parties and high summer teas.

As I look through my window, what do I see?
Rows of houses, no sign of a tree,
Where once green fields and valleys lay,
Hordes of cars cram the motorway,
Bins overflowing, people don't care,
They throw down rubbish anywhere.
England, oh England, where has it gone?
The quiet peace I used to gaze upon.

The simple pleasures all washed away,
On a timeless tide of violence today.
A moody madness grips the heart
And terror stalks where twilight shadows dart.
Tall tower blocks seem to lean and sway
To the pulsing beat of life today.
Nowhere to run, nowhere to hide
It engulfs us all in its surging tide.
England, oh England, where has it gone?
The quiet peace I gazed upon.

Margot

Southall, The Little Bombay In Ealing

My people have come far and near
Some have come because of persecution, better life
Above all, to acquire knowledge
I am rich because my people believe in working
My streets are full of shops and kiosks because my people believe in trading
and majority are family owned businesses
I have made my name because of my dominant culture
I am colourful and vibrant
The colours can be seen ranging from turbans, apparels, regalia, bedding,
bangles and in foods
Oh! You cannot walk on my major streets and not spot my distinguished,
remarkable decorated car either standing or roaming
The aromas from food especially curry soups, stew, chicken, fish, chips and
stir fries cannot be forgotten
My known language has become alienated on all streets and roads of Southall
I have no gold, silver and copper mines but my street is full of gold, silver and
copper
I have no vegetables or fruit plantations but my people are vegetarians
My garment factories sell well, because my people know how to use them and
attract all walks of life
My people are called diamonds because they sparkle and shine all the time
You will starve and kill my people when you banned the selling of British whole
milk and sweets because my people have sweet teeth and love for milk
You do not need to starve or stress yourself to cook food, or need some
booster for appetites; I have many restaurants and cafés all around my streets
In the night, our major streets are like Oxford Street, full of lights, all sorts
of cars, limousine, Lamborghini, Porsche, Mercedes, BMW, Peugeot, Ford,
Renault and others
Cannot also miss our youth rampaging with their girlfriends and boyfriends on
our streets in the night
For some people, the nightfall is their party time and celebrations
Grandfathers and grandmothers are the backbone of our children's
upbringing and care and could see them in all our schools
Last but not least, children grow up and emulate their parents

Agatha Haizel

No Place Like Home

First of all my name is Jill,
I live in a place called Studd Hill.
It's a small private estate almost in Herne Bay
with a community hall, to have your say,
Although the roads are concrete, some are bumpy and unmade,
So money raised from hall events, help for tarmac to be laid.
Coffee mornings, bingo, quiz nights, jumbles and even a band,
Craft days, Elvis nights and an open bar, where residents can get canned!
We are only five minutes walk from the promenade and sea,
Lovely for dog walking, cycling, swimming and a car park – that's free!

When we were kids and you were able to travel on buses alone
And stay out all day roaming the streets, without a mobile phone,
My friend Diana and I used to fish off the end of Herne Bay pier,
Go roller skating and watch wrestling, was great as the bus stop was near.
The penny slot machines opposite used to give us endless fun
Then have ice cream with a flake in and sit on the beach in the sun.
There used to be a boating pool just before the entrance to the estate,
At times it was so busy to hire a boat, we would have to wait.

Studd Hill used to be holiday homes, then the army took control in 1916
Using the area for training purposes, some of the huts can still be seen,
Once war was over, new builds took over from holiday homes,
Some huge with palm trees, some small with garden gnomes.
All the roads on the estate are named after makes of old cars,
At the entrances there are weight restriction signs with barriers and bars,
This is to save the roads from unnecessary weight and stress,
Sadly there are a handful of people though, that really couldn't care less.
It's nice being on Studd Hill where majority of people wave or say hi
People from Whitstable say, you moved to Studd Hill but why?
Because people are friendly, with a nearby bus stop and convenient store,
The sea round the corner, the town less than a mile, I couldn't ask for more.

Jill Weightman

A Great Place To Live

The sound of the birds welcoming the dawn
The rising sun, blue skies and cloudy days
Occasional thunderstorms and rain to water the earth

The early morning milkman, as he delivers the milk
The local postman, delivering the mail

Family life, as we rise to face the day ahead
Breakfast and the first cup of the day
Rustled hair and sleepy eyes
A kiss and cuddle!

A wash and brush up, a change of clothes
Work and play, people bustling about their tasks
Mothers or fathers taking their children to school
Walks in the countryside or cycling down country lanes

Or, perhaps a leisurely drive to the seaside
Sand dune strolls, making sandcastles
A swim or a paddle, beach combing

Riverside walks along unpolluted rivers
Traditional oak beamed pubs and Sunday roasts
Boating and duck ponds
Saving your bread, to feed the ducks

Bees buzzing as they flit from flower to flower
Scented roses and honeysuckle
Ants tracing little trails amongst the plants
The breeze caressing the leaves, of rustling trees

Rolling hills, mountains and lovely views
Lakes and rivers
The rustic charm of country scenes
Appreciating nature and all its glory

The National Trust and British Heritage
Historic buildings in classic architectural styles and designs
Thoughtful planning and conservation
British traditions and culture, going back generations

Community craft groups and country fairs
Farming life, woolly sheep and little lambs
Cattle and horses, munching on hay

Quaint local shops with beautiful window displays
Local markets, selling home-grown produce
Cobbled streets and nearby parks

Chatting, over a cup of tea, with our neighbours
Kind thoughts and gentle hearts.

Helen Vipond

North East, Northumberland

The beauty of Northumberland, no one can deny.
Come for a visit, you'll not believe your eyes.
Stunning coastal beaches, seaside sarnies, what a treat.
Love the feeling of the sand on your feet.

A stroll along the North East coast, a day you won't forget.
Welcomed by the locals, 'Why aye, nee botha pet!'
Bamburgh Castle, Lindisfarne and many more to see.
A stroll along our beautiful coast can make you feel so free.

The seahouses, harbours, fishermen in the sea.
A happy place to visit, I'm sure you'll agree.

The contemporary Alnwick Gardens, the rural beauty of Alnmouth.
All as stunning as the places we visit in the south.

Delicious Craster crab, sand dunes at Druridge Bay,
Rock pools where the kids can play,
Fish and chips at Seaton Sluice, Whitley Bay.

St Mary's lighthouse, a picturesque postcard of your stay.
The family gathered round on a warm summer's day.

Sandcastles, amusements, Seaton Delaval ice cream,
Crazy golf, surfing the waves, fishing nets in the streams.

The North East, Northumberland, a region to be proud.
So much on our doorstep, we're shouting it out loud,
'Come and visit us, nee matta where ya from,'
A warm welcome waiting for each and every one.

Michelle Barr

Gateshead: A Place To Live

In May 1958 I arrived, without warning or a sign,
My mother was doing the washing, hanging the clothes onto the line,
Suddenly she felt water, trickling slowly down her legs,
The shock was so great for her, she dropped the washing and the pegs,
The pains they came quickly, labour established without doubt,
My dad he was at his work, and my grandmother had gone out,
I was three weeks too early, so nothing had been prepared,
The midwife and my gran arrived, and my delivery they shared,
I came into the world screaming, put straight onto the breast,
My mother was exhausted, she needed plenty care and rest,

I was the second of four daughters, all healthy and very bright,
Our parents they both loved us, even though money was very tight,
We were born in the town of Gateshead, lived in a one-bedroomed flat,
The six of us together, barely room to swing a cat,
The toilet it was outside, the bath hung in the hall,
It came out on Friday, the same water used for all,
'Don't throw the baby out with the bathwater,' my mother used to say,
Especially after a few baths, as the water turned dirty grey,
We came from a large Catholic family, my mother was one of ten,
The matriarch was my grandmother, respected by both the women and the
men,

Gateshead was a working-class area, with a high street full of bars,
There were trams that took us to Newcastle, we never needed cars,
We shopped at the Co-Op, the dividend gave us treats,
It was not very often, that our mother bought us sweets,
Shepherd's was the posh shop, where often we used to wander,
My dad sometimes bought us a toy, but there was little money to squander,
On Sundays we walked to the Quay Side, we had Sarsaparilla to drink,
We always wore our Sunday best, four little girls dressed in pink,
On weekdays we went to Saltwell Park, the best without a doubt,
The Maze Lake and Animal Corner, we played until worn out,

'Gateshead is the dirty back lane to Newcastle,' Dr Johnson had stated,
But he could have seen Gateshead develop, if only he had waited,
From the breweries to mining, from the Millennium to the Sage,
From the Shipley to the Baltic, our art is all the rage,
The Jewish community settled here, of that we are so proud,
Our football team have flourished, now drawing quite a crowd,
Our flower festival is legendary, the stadium has international fame,

The Metro Centre has everything, shopping will never be the same,
To live on Gateshead river banks, is what many now desire,
To see the Tyne and its bridges, is a view that will never tire,

A place to live is all we need, they say, 'What's in a name?'
But I am proud to have been born in Gateshead, to die here is my aim,
I live here still even though, I have travelled far and wide,
Everywhere I have roamed, I speak of Gateshead with such pride,
The one-bedroomed flat where I was born, it is no longer there,
A police station stands on that site, but my street name it does bear,
Gateshead has changed much over the years, but the people remain the same,
It is not the town that has made history, it is the people who create its fame,
It is true what they say, believe it if you can,
'You can take the man out of Gateshead, but you will never take Gateshead out of the man'.

Maria Barrell

Bank Holiday

Knobbly-kneed children don wetsuits behind rainbow-coloured windshields,
shrieking with shock as they jump and splash in the icy aqua;
teeth chattering under stark blue sky.

Feet protected from sandy gravel by flip-flops and Crocs.
Skimmed stones and plopped pebbles reclaimed
by the waves, murmuring their secrets as they retreat into the deep.

Silent, swan-like sail boats drift by on the breeze
while jet skis growl, leaving white horses in their wake and
kayakers sweep away tension with each gentle stroke.

Home-made foiled-wrapped sandwiches are munched.
Scents of sea-salt, seaweed, suncream and bitter coffee from faithful old
flasks pervade as precious time together is enjoyed and family memories are made.

Sigrid Marceau

Living In England

(And What That Means To Me)

I want to try and tell you about my favourite place on Earth
You might think I'm slightly biased, as it's the country of my birth
But for oh so many reasons, it means the world to me
There is no doubt about it, it's the only place to be

A culture so rich and varied, and these days quite diverse
So much creativity, whether through art, or song or verse
We've given the world some shining stars, a few are mentioned here
Elgar, The Beatles, Turner, Dickens, and of course Mr Shakespeare

Fried egg and bacon, cups of tea and beautiful rolling hills
We talk about the weather, and sing of our iconic mills
Some say that we're eccentric, but we don't mind a jot
Our unique sense of humour has seen us through a lot

Old pubs with real ale, and log fires that burn so bright
Exhibits in museums, for sore eyes, such a sight
Sunday afternoon drives, and sensational brass bands
Sightseeing in London, or a day on Blackpool Sands

Roast beef and Yorkshire pud, and strolling through the park
Barbecues in the garden, and fireworks when it's dark
When it comes to raising money, we're up there with the best
We'll shave our hair, jump out of planes, or sing and dance, and jest

We are a sporting nation, and football is our game
With every win, or loss, or draw, the fervour is the same
We turn out in our thousands, and invest our heart and soul
Cheer and chant until we're hoarse, and crave that winning goal

We've played our part in history, whether rich or poor
Not all of it we're proud of, but of one thing I am sure
That the people of this land are both resilient and true
However tough the going gets, together we pull through

There's such outstanding beauty at every twist and turn
Each time I go away, it is for this place that I yearn
For nowhere else could ever touch my heart in the same way
Home sweet home is England, and this is where I want to stay

Jenny Quigley

Coming Home

I grew up overseas
In a land of sunshine, dust
And waving palm trees
And then I moved to England
In January.

Stark, black, bare trees supporting
Grey skies pressing down
On sodden mud and grass so
Green it hurt my eyes.
And the constant chill
I felt ill.

Spring finally arrived and the sky showed blue.
Flowers and blossom gave
The dullness a brighter hue.
The mud dried away and leaves grew on trees
Suddenly all was green
Closing in, so verdant, so alive.

It's twenty years since I moved here.
Sometimes it seems forever.
I've come to love the changing seasons
The spring blossoms, gentle summer sun, windy autumn
And stark, bare winter.
This is my home now
I'm here to stay.

But sometimes I remember
My youth – the non-stop sunshine
The heat, the sea, the openness of it all,
And I look outside
At the sparrows
Squabbling in the honeysuckle over a fatball.
I'm home.

Kym Wheeler

An English Glade

The morning dew covers the long grass
In the glade where fairies once danced.
As the scent of the wild hawthorn perfumes the still air
The brook sparkles in the early morning light,
As it tumbles down over rocks of quartz.
And a fawn breaks cover to taste the magic water
As a jay cries in the trees and butterflies dance.
Life returns to the ground as the earth relishes its veins
After winter's hibernation ends.
Dandelion parasols blow through the misty air
As they travel to a new home, a new birth.

No more the toil of man, just a gentle breeze
As it sways the tall grasses with wild garlic.
A bluebell bends, oh so slightly, in calmness
When the sun's rays break through giving honey shimmers,
The buzz of the bumblebee as they hover over the buttercups
Moves the stillness and sends ripples.
And I lie there to feel it course through my blood
And become as one with the nature god's kingdom.
As it engulfs my mind and I sink into its heaven
Long gone from the toil of the world
As I leave all behind.

Steve Uttley

Step Short

Folkestone Town is where I live,
It featured in the war,
The Road of Remembrance and the Leas,
Are what the soldiers saw.

Millions of men heard the officer cry,
'Step Short' and ready the 'slope',
Knowing that thousands of them may die,
It didn't deter their hope.

They boarded the ships to sail to France,
Their future was never secure,
Hoping to get just one last chance,
Of the glistening Folkestone shore.

One hundred years on,
An arch is to be built,
Remembering the men that have gone,
Who gave their lives right up to the hilt
And on those we depended upon.

Prince Harry arrives on August the Fourth,
To unveil the tribute 'Step Short',
He's in the town to follow the path,
Of the men that went before.

Nikki Robinson

Great Britain

I may not have much money
Or earn a load of dosh
Where I live isn't perfect
In fact, I'm not that posh
But home is where the heart is
It's always been that way
For I'm a British citizen
Of that, I'm proud to say
I've never had a passport
I've never felt the need
To travel the world over
I'm from a British seed
Content with being British
I live
The best I can
In love, peace and harmony
Helping my fellow man
The beauty of this land of ours
Is way beyond compare
What nature creates
For Britain
Is as good as anywhere
Be thankful for the things you have
Be proud of where you live
Forget about the greed and wars
Give what
You have to give
For every good deed actioned
Along our earthly way
Means Britain will be great until
We live our final day.

Jennifer Melbourne

Meditation On Rutland

So often I've wandered their beauty unending,
The byways of Rutland when summer has flown;
And grieved at its passing with grey mist descending
While leaves into thick coloured carpets are blown.

The sorrow I feel as the seasons are passing
Reflecting a life that all but now spent,
Is harder to bear as the years are now massing
And old age confirms that our youth is just lent.

The churchyard I stop at compounds this great sadness
As there on its tombstones, most faded away,
Are memories of loved ones, recalled with such gladness,
With no one to tend them with this bleak autumn day.

For time has eroded, in slow even paces,
The hovels of surfs and the castles of kings,
Till nothing is left but occasional traces
In fields where the mistle thrush sings.

Perhaps they all too had their fears, that proved groundless,
For the uncertain future their children must face,
But ours is an age when destruction is boundless.
They knew not the terror of life's ruthless pace

Where many now live for a life of distraction
That numbs all their senses, and calms the real dread
Of the horror or hate and its hideous reaction
That leaves sometimes no one to bury the dead,

In vain do the voices of reason shout warning,
But their message is drowned in an ocean of greed,
For few will believe that the holocaust dawning
Has been caused by all those that take more than they need.

Yet, when I consider life's splendour abounding
This moment in time seems like only a game,
Played out on a voyage where we each take our sounding,
But a thousand years hence will it still be the same?

Januarius

The Wanderer's Return

The sea was rough, the sky was black.
No stars shone in the heavens that night.
But on the sombre shore in little groups,
Like glow worms in the dark, there twinkled lights.
Thank God! I thought, I'm back.

From fields afar, where forests stretched
Amongst a thousand secret lakes.
Barren plains and mountains high,
As far as eyes could see
And cities strange with cultures alien to me.

To where my heart will always be,
A gentle place, where wanderers rest,
By rippling streams, and village greens
Where men in white put on a show
With bats of crafted willow.
And churchyards with their headstones row on row,
That mark the bones and ashes of those gone before.
Who knows what ancient tales they'd tell,
Were they alive and not at rest,
Of life and death and hell.
And soon amongst their number, my own will add one more,
So say the grand old bells that toll death's knell.

So as once more I place my feet
Upon this hallowed shore.
In this, my final port of call,
I'll seek those things most dear to me.
The music in the concert hall,
The cottage with a roof of thatch,
Logs burning on an open grate.
A pint of foaming ale and fish and chips,
In some old pub amongst the company of mates.
But most of all our family and loving wife
Who stood by me despite my wayward care
And still awaits, the final years to share -
The best years of our life.

Ben Corde

Carlisle To Settle

Setting off we sally forth
Along the Eden Valley

But soon the engine shows
Its mettle and puffs
Asthmatically to Dent
Then, taking breath, free falls.

For many miles our eyes
Take in the dappled light
Especially beyond
Each bravely navvied night.

We venture proudly over viaducts
Slink slyly through the cuttings
From Appleby
To Ribblehead and Settle.

Meanwhile at each encounter
The sheep and horses shy away.
Rabbits in profusion
Scud swiftly in confusion.

All against a fluid backcloth
Of speeding fluffy clouds
Tipped by the setting sun
In an early autumn sky.

Graham Waring

Bonnie Scotland

Down to earth and friendly folk with our own
Cheeky banter and good auld jokes
Tattie scone and Irn Bru, haggis and neeps
To name a few.
Glasgow, Edinburgh and Inverness just some of our great cities
To see places to relax and stay or just for dinner or tea
Museums and castles with breathtaking views
With our own Loch Ness monster who gets in the news.

Our weather with all the seasons in one day,
Rain, hail and shine come our way.
But it never dampens our spirits, we are a nation that fly our satire
Flag high welcoming visitors from all over the world making them feel at home
They never want to stay goodbye.

So think again before you fly off yonder and come and visit Scotland
And have a ponder, stay and enjoy the Celtic way because
Scotland the brave is here to stay.

Irene Burns

Summer In England, Aged Twelve

The sun at the tip of a scream -
August feral hot and dizzy with sin
then dusk starved to a bark

and as frost worms a sly root
we bite the shudder
waiting for light to seed,

for a skylark to lift the wind
on mud-crazed puddles,
tarmac bubbling empty miles.

Ian Clarke

Bidston Hill – A Walk In The Rain

A walk in the rain,
All alone with your thoughts,
In the forest,
At the top of the hill.

Pine trees and birch,
Rhododendrons and ferns,
Bramble, thistle and holly.

To reminisce,
Of the times you have had.
The good times, the bad times,
The happy times, the sad.

A walk in the rain,
All alone with your thoughts,
In the forest,
At the top of the hill.

Guppyman

An Ode To Bradford

We never move far away,
This collective 'we'.
The homeland, engraved into our hardened minds,
We never go far.

Terrorised streets fuelled by drugs gangs,
Serial killers made this place their home.
Racial hatred blooms in this place,
But we never move far away.

Scorched-out buildings, products of riots
Still stand, echoes of mini-warfare.
Rubbish, parts of forgotten lives, litters the streets.
But something makes us keep coming back.
We never move far away.
This is the homeland.

Jo Merritt

The Iron Mask

Post nuclear war, industrial zone,
The landscape mimics an apocalyptic scene.
Iron and concrete stretching afar
Separated only by the River of Steel.

The town reaches out to housing estates,
Roof upon roof; UPVC mould.
No trees grow on this concrete lawn
Only bricks and pots of council gold.

Urban conurbations built on industry past,
Smoggies labelled amidst polluted clouds,
Strangers can't see through the darkened mass,
Of a town surrounded by beauty abound.

Three mile to the east and the seaside emerges
Four mile to the south and hills line the sky,
One mile to the west and forests grow wild
Cathedrals and castles in the north lie.

The industry hides a secret escape
Camouflaged in steel in a mysterious cloud,
A secluded haven wearing an iron mask
Of a north eastern nirvana in an industrial shroud.

Lesley D'Arcy

Yorkshire And Me

Bin oop north some time now – me
I like it though – me
A've kept me southern accent though – me
Still struggle to understand the dialect – like
Aye, Yorkshire hasn't affected me

Paul Franklin

The English Rose

Nature's parable is the rose
Where beauty with pain entwines,
Burgeoning blossoms atop thorny stems
Ready to repel fumbling fingers.
Reverence brings its own rewards:
To inhale the dizzying scent, bow your head,
Hold back, riveted by the richness of hue,
Fresher than fresco.
Gaze upon its delicate whorls
Whereon Cellinis have tried their art,
Their icons paling beside the ardent blooms.
Virginal and seductive are those buds
Opening shyly and moistly to the sun's sweet caress.
Velvet to the touch their melting petals,
Full blooms are wenches, fully ripe at their peak.
Diffidence surfaces as the petals spread and lose their sheen;
Bereft of flowers, saw-edged teeth stand starkly menacing.
Memory, recoiling from raw reality,
Glorifies the fading pleasures
Until the masquerade revels anew.

Patricia Bruce

Malling In Bloom

The village I live in is full of wonder
The many pubs with their tales of happiness and woe
Where dreams are made and lost and friends get together, a place they all go
Surrounded by fields full of colour and life
And the many churches where woman becomes wife
A few schools teaching the kids to prosper and learn
While in little houses the log fires burn
But the best thing about my village is those dear to me
My talented beautiful wife Maureen and loving family
Our many pets of many different breeds
And all the love they will ever need

Stephen Black

Southrepps

Crooked as old teeth, broken,
Random spaced,
Weather-worn with spots of moss.
Long neglected gravestones.
Memories rooted in a century past of
A quiet Norfolk churchyard.
Square-towered and solid
The grey stone of St James'
Where once the faithful people of the village
Filled the pews to quench their souls.

This stormy summer Sunday we stroll
Between the fading epitaphs.
Albert, Edward, Ernie with
Mary, Ethel, Annie, engraved
Above or below
Depending on who first met earth.
Words for lost loved fathers.
Prayers for mothers, sons and daughters.

Leaving the graveyard now
We wander down Church Lane to find,
On all sides, the bygone lives.
Past the old Post Office,
The house where blacksmith tapped and hammered,
Shaped the metal on the anvil.
The barn of the harness-maker,
The sweet shop, district nurse and baker.

Now at the Vernon Arms
We quench our thirsts.
This is where we stop to gather
To put the world to rights and mutter.
Untroubled if our final bones
Will be buried at the top of the lane
In the mouth of Heaven.

Pat Barber

The Great River

Canoe floats like a leaf
Reflections in the water
Sunlight, leaf, bird,
Chameleon river watches.

White fish, blue water
Dives straight down,
Evening shadows cross river
Breeze in seed grass.

Being out there
Thinking about times past
Times to come
And about today.

Smoking river moves
Across land, wings rise
Millions of mayfly, born,
Mate, lay and die.

Canoe moves through water
Hyacinth purple in sunlight
Saucer leaves hold dew
Diamonds dance in little breeze

Slow wings through mist
Canoe noses into silence
Trees come, go like ghosts
Into birth of the river.

Birds twirling, circling,
Tornado wings to roost
In reflections red, yellow, brown,
In still, calm river water.

Teta

Jerusalem

Great Britain is my Jerusalem,
in this fair land of milk and honey, where I've set down roots.
This tiny Hampshire village is protected by an army garrison,
we share a border with Wiltshire.
Spring in Hampshire countryside is so lush and vibrant,
a place where ancient history drips out of its chalk soil.
Ancient warriors lie under towering trees,
Saxon, Roman, Norman, Celts, not forgetting the Vikings.
Warriors fought for every inch of ground,
so precious to them, and now priceless to us.
Serenaded by arias of birdsong, their spirits are still here,
and rise up in the form of swirling mists.
We enjoy the same air that they did decades ago,
our life so peaceful, theirs was not.
In total wonderment of our ancestors,
who were they, and of which creed and faith?
Humanity in all its glory runs through our veins,
our kin sleep soundly beneath the soil.

In these modern times HRH Prince Charles,
is involved in protecting our green meadows.
His help is a guardian to the vast range of wildlife,
and wild flora that insects and animals need and share.
A comfort to know that someone at the top of the tree,
is taking an interest, and his work is so valuable to young and old.
MOD ground for conservation, runs from the tip to toe of our land,
I love this land; no other in the world can ever shine a light to our home.
This land where no warrior will feel shame when asking for help,
no jewel sparkles or shines as bright as Our Golden Jubilee sovereign.
If I could change a thing about Britain I would not,
God set me down in Britain's fair land forever.
And did those feet in ancient times,
walk upon England's pleasant land?

Starling

We Are Lucky

We are lucky, living here, in this our England
When we awake we see a lovely day that dawns,
Sometimes blue, where the clouds have not yet gathered
Sometimes grey, appearing sad and most forlorn.

But we are free to rise up slowly from our slumber
And discard the soft warm shackles of our bed,
Hear our inner song rise slowly up to Heaven
Or just smile about our daily plans, instead.

We have no fear of blackened missiles in our skies
We can walk safe along our streets, so green and lush
Meeting neighbours with a greeting loud and happy
We have no need to run, no quiet footsteps in a rush.

We take for granted all the colours of our landscape
As the season rolls from spring to summertime
We have no need to worry that our home will still be here
When we once again return, to enjoy food and some good wine.

We sometimes cry when we are happy or we're blue
But grief lingers not within our soul, to long decay
We can embrace our sad emotions yet know our fellow man
Will respond to all our needs in a kind and friendly way.

Yes we are lucky, living here, in this our England
Where the terror borne of bombs does not hold sway,
Where the life that we can live, is the one that we can choose
Not imposed or forced upon us by unnatural affray.

Sandra Griesbach

England

Where bobbies walked down the streets in twos
and one can catch the train at Waterloo
to travel down to see the Purbeck Views
and later saunter on to visit Poole

In English hills and English downs
where Hardy wrote and Tess sat down
where Shakespeare wrote and Elliot too
where Bacon wrote his bible free
and Tolpuddle martyrs talked of liberty

Where Lawrence Shaw wrote on Clouds Hill
Brunel created bridges to span the sea
whilst children played their game before their tea
here where church and manor house resides
alongsides the sandy beaches and the roaring tides

There's Forests New and Sherwood too
even Buffalo Bill came to ride his show at Poole
theres EastEnders and Coronation Street
all of the kindest people you'd want to meet

The Brummy lad and Geordie crew
the Brownsea Island scouts at Poole
the rose of Kent and Liverpool
the Beatles and the Mersey too

The trains of steam at Swanage Town
the Malvern Hills springs
you can drink the pure water down
the Buck house of Queen and Kings
the palaces and buskers that play and sing

The swans and open country lanes
the dips and dales
the sights and smells
then the journey up to Tunbridge Wells

The fields of corn and wheat and rye
where the village postmen pass you by
the football lads and cricketers
the history and the Lady Diane tears

The brooks and rivers
the trains and boats
the island race
the mix of pace and totes

St George and the dragon and George Orwell
the Houses of Parliament and Orson Wells
the crowds, the tourists and the cup of tea
the battles won, the victory.

Raymond Wills

My Wales

My Wales
A new home to my family
How it's welcomed me.

Wales of school friends
Wales of strange
Mysterious weather
Wales of rain
Of history
Of new people and places
And houses in rows.

Wales of symbols
Roaring red dragons
Buttery yellow daffodils
And strange words.

Wales

My new home.

Crimson Rose

Diving In St Bride's Bay

Sunshine slips from the shoulder of summer
Like a shawl to the floor
Early autumn light brushes the cliffs to
Soften sharp shadows

The ungracious gulls are poor company today,
Protesting the intrusion
Of the divers, inching over the dribbling stones
Like the grey ocean

Which picks at the stitches of the neoprene skin
Protecting our innards,
Till it falls apart and the sea comes in,
Chilling the bones

Diving in the crescent arms of the bay
Those unruly waters
Toss our intentions, playing marbles
With the pebbles

The divers drift in the dirty brown depths,
Finding their peace
Until just enough air remains in the tank
To break the surface

We rise to the slate grey of open waters
Through a forest of olive kelp;
Until we lay on the seabed I thought nothing
Was as cold as silence.

Drew Ridley-Siegert

Rum Lot The English

Patient, cautious, tolerant folks
Long-suffering sometimes stroppy blokes
Condescending, God's chosen race
Settling here from all over the place.

Marmite-munching, carrot-crunching,
Flat cap wearing, often swearing,
Jacket potatoes, shepherd's pie,
Chicken korma, old school tie.

Country lanes, the driving rain,
The lasting pain of a go-slow train,
The glory of this island's races,
Rows of smiling soggy faces.

Seen at squash and the odd golf course,
On a country hack with a knackered horse,
Followed up by fresh cream teas,
Swallowed with the greatest ease.

More Monty Python than Shakespeare and Milton
Less like Cheddar than strong smelling Stilton.
The whole world wants to be English you see,
So why in Heaven's name don't we!

Vince Horsman

Home Is There Somehow

Awoken in the mist from the great River Tyne
This city is a cracker
But it's certainly no mine.
I'm used to the Haggis, the neaps and a tattie
No the brown ale that's here
Or the bread they call Stottie.

A mean aye I love it noo that I've moved down south
They don't understand a word out of ma mouth
I can git away with murder when I talk too quick
Just blabber on a sentence they look at me like I'm thick.

But I think of hame and my heart fills wae pride
Of the pipes and the Saltire and the great River Clyde.
Wearing a kilt whit the English, they call a skirt.
Rolling aboot as a bairn in the dirt
Watchin' the fitbaw cheering yir team
No black and white there, just the blue and the green.

This passion we have is heard all around
From the rusty peseta, to the great British pound.
Aye we argue but it's all a bit of banter
like the local politicians who love a good ranter.

We drink too much and shout too loud
We love all our gardens and sing in the crowds.
We're small remember but bravest of the brave
Champions of the excuses for the way we behave.

But when it comes down to it
We're all just the same
Just living in the north of the country
Just guts and no shame.

We laugh, we fight, we care, we joke
After long days at work we love a gid soak.
Use have your Geordies and we have our Jocks.
The cities are founded by workers in docks.

I am proud of where I am and I've been made felt at hame.
I might even get round to St James fir a game.
I mean I'll keep my Rs rolling in my speech and so forth
But home is here somehow . . . at least I'm still in the north.

Bryan Johnson Mc

Village Tree

We are grown
from the roots
of this little place,
my friends,
the bowels,
of the grave,
the deposit
of our genes.

We are the indigenous,
the core,
come up through
the trees
very centre,
grown into the leaves,
inhaled by the sky
and lifted upwards
until we reach
the warmth of freedom
and the path
of our ancestors.

We will nourish eternity
with our spirits.

Sally Plumb

Kittlingbourne

Kittlingbourne, Kittlingbourne.
Sometimes lush, sometimes worn.
Overseeing mill and plough,
From the splendour of the brow.

Kittlingbourne, Kittlingbourne.
Antidote when you're forlorn.
Overriding stress and strain,
Via vista and terrain.

Kittlingbourne, Kittlingbourne.
Steadfast as the early morn.
Overlooking field and hills,
Keeper of a view that thrills.

Paul Kelly

Pathways In Hulme

I love these old alleys, shopping-crowd freed;
ginnels, snickets, film sets for a Dickens.
Read the rubbish: dark tights, torn syringe,
traces of costly, smoke-shared parties.

I tap to rhythms of pop-songs-on-the-brain
past gravel where only I see Zen abstracts,
through an empty square with one stone dolphin -
behind re-clad blocks to a white bridge for walkers;
backpack frees thoughts, while rain douses my hat.

I ferret out shady lanes for rambling near
my canal, its marina barging with other lives,
and a secret path thrusting holly, huge ferns -
city's wild pretence at being elsewhere.

Olga Kenyon

Hoe!

A winding road leads up the Hoe
Past striped tower, an empty hour.
An emptied bandstand alone, forlorn -
Through a monument or other – stone solid through,
Grey grumpy church flying its banner of
Defiance of
Honour scared, and destroyed
Of stubbornness
Resolved
To stand; in front of an abstract
Of convergence as
Shoppers and milkmen and postmen,
Sailors and artists,
Poets and markets must make hay while

                                                            Up

All the way
All the way

                                                            Down

The stripy red tower stands proud – around and around.
It's a father of water that surrounds ships and pools guiding a light far into the
night
Of churches and steeples and people asleep in their beds
Resting their heads in a place that is quiet,
Shush! Sleepyheads.

Caro Bushnell

Wish You'd Gone Into London

I wish you'd gone into London with me,
Past all the winters,
And the frosted park
That used to fill with children
Till the dark came back.

I wish you'd gone into London with me.
Through Christmas lights to outskirt homes
Where quiet people reading rhyme
In circles sat.

Wish all my lifetimes
They had let you step through,
Past theatre queues and stone-lioned squares,
And we rode in winter.

Wish up from the wintry lawn we had gone,
Past the hem of London,
Our breath like smoke,
East to the raucous chorus of pubs,
The playground where infants
Squealed in their playtime,
And you at my side by slushy kerbs.

Oh all those kerbs I tilted on,
Stood in a storm on,
With you ever absent,
And clouds so low they scarfed my neck.

Where I was small on pavements
Before you were born,
Below a big river
The morning tugs chugged on.

Wish gone with me you had
And gladly left the sunny suburb
Behind in the past
When we started out.

Up to the murky river of the city,
When wreaths of cold
Made office girls run.

There where once a child of Spain,
Complaining in Angel,
Bicycle rode and waved her hand,
Or scorned my greeting beyond his wall,
A painter who sailed from far Japan.

Near still and chimeless bells of Bow,
When pigeons pecked at rainy bread,
Where once I yearned in chilly rags
And waited on the dark to pass,

Getting nowhere in a drizzle,
Over east-end puddles stepping,
And, for a cradle, crazily curling
In the massive park of grass.

It was sad that you couldn't come,
To the waiting lanes,
Metropolitan sun,
To one of those worlds I would have had you step through,
Where lovers left by the wide park path.

As I still roved,
The late mist breathing
In the street and through the railings,
As all the children abed lay hailing
The coming of the stars.

Kevin Ryan

Yearnings

Oh for a frosty English morn with the aged grass bent low beneath,
For a bright clear sunlit dawn with the shadows wide and drawn.
Oh for the echoing call of a shouting pheasant sounding o'er the vale,
For the linnet robin and soaring lark, and the peace of an English park.

Oh for the breath of a scent-filled spring, with the blossoms rich and full.
For the smell of new mown hay on a balmy evening at the close of day.
Oh for my home, my land of birth, with the soils so rich and good.
And for the Ford the Country Fare, the Comradeship and the Care.

Oh for meadow field and tea, with heads of corn in windswept sway.
For the plough'ed furrow straight and true, and growth fresh and new.
Oh for the welcome of a wood log fire, with dancing flames to ignite my
dreams.
For succulent sirloin Sunday roast, and butter and eggs with marmalade and
toast.

Oh for my green and verdant land with weeping willow and majestic oak.
For the sound of a crowing cock, and the ticking of an old grandfather clock.
Oh for a pint in an English pub with crisps and peanuts in a bowl to hand
Oh for the sound of leather on bat, and the gentle purring of a contented cat.

Peter Hewett

Wonders Of The World

Stare at the highest mountain
Or just Southend pleasure pier
Gaze at the stars on a clear night
Or just Blackpool illuminations
Admire the pyramids of Egypt
Or the gates of Buckingham Palace
Discover exotic plants and animals
Or a small fish in your local pond
Taste food all over the world
Or just have bangers and mash
All of these wonders in the world
Or just lie in bed and watch you sleep.

Adam Carter

Reflections

The River Derwent with its moods,
Reflects the history
Of Belper's mills and working class
And spinning industry.
Terraced rows of brick-built homes
Where mill workers once dwelt,
Reflect the people from the past,
Whose ghosts can still be felt.
Peregrines fly from the mill,
Reflections in their eye,
Of finding prey to feed their young
Left in their nest up high.
The River Gardens set below,
With flowerbeds and grass,
Has bandstand to reflect the mood
Of live bands and of brass.
With children playing on the swings
And wooden boats to oar,
The river, is a lovely place
To reflect, and explore.
A small town with its local shops
And stone-paved marketplace,
Reflects a warmth to everyone
Who shops and fills its space.

Linda Knight

Northern Carnival – The Dancers

Tippy-toe tap down the lane, through the square,
Come Stacey and Tracy and Kylie and Clare
And Gemma and Emma and Zoe and Faye
And Sharon and Karen on Carnival Day.
Hordes upon hordes of them tippy-toe tapping,
A clatter that's echoed by satisfied clapping
Of mothers admiring their babes on parade,
Kaleidoscope-costumed and fondly displayed;
In Day-Glo chemises of market-stall satin
Embellished with flounces Americo-Latin,
Or powder puff tutus on pigeon-toed poppets:
A crecheful of open-eyed, mystified moppets.
Counterfeit bunnies, with scuts proudly fluffy
And ears at attention, queue up at the buffet.
Giggling gaggles of nondescript dickies,
With beaks round their faces, munch chocolate bickies.
Tacky confections of overdone cuteness
Rub shoulders with gear whose designer's astuteness
Avoided the precious, achieving the witty;
A welcome relief amid prosaic pretty.
Steams of bright tinsel, they flow on the field
And wait to have tippy-tap talents revealed.

Tappy-tap thump, as they hammer the boards.
Come fully grown versions of hordes upon hordes.
There's Marlene and Carole and Pam and Charmaine;
Whose bra strap elastic is feeling the strain;
And big-bottomed Beryl, unsuitably dressed:
In fishnets and ciré she's not at her best.
With bosoms a-bounce and their faces aglow
And visible panty lines firmly on show,
As social phenomena they are entrancing:
Such bulk so bedizened and merrily dancing.
The stage creaks and booms as their energy peaks
And seismograph readings are jiggered for weeks.
While robbers flee cops, giving truncheons an airing,
And vamps rashly shimmy, their fantasies glaring;
As gun-slinging cowgirls in make-believe leathers
Chase past-their-best Injuns in war-paint and feathers;
The Castanet Cuties and Cha-Cha-Cha Charmers

And Rock 'n' Roll Rainbows and Folderol Farmers
Thump, thump, tappy-thump, in bizarre cavalcade,
Till toes and heels thunder their last cannonade.
Then the plumes go to roost till a month from today,
When a neighbouring town holds its Carnival Day.

Freda Bunce

From This Isle

Albion erupts in crowns, sceptres, churches, holy woods burning with
incantations.
Thank you, Odysseus, for burning down Troy;
Setting adrift Aeneus, who gripped Rome in his gauntlet,
Whom spawned Brutus,
Whose feet clomped upon this isle, alone and adrift.

'Give me your hand, Arthur,'
And so sprouts Avalon, streaming across the land.
These hills are more ancient than you Merlin.
The language only appears to crumble;
It pulses underneath
Like a heady, tumultuous organ;
It ruptures through Latin,
The soft, amorphic, the dough spread across the globe.

We know cold. Heat.
We know the forests like the stumps of our beards,
Like the hair on our head;
We *are* the hills, we *are* the trees,
We were these things,
Long before Brutus, Arthur, Caesar,
Hadrada, William, Henry, George,
Captain Swing, Ned Ludd,
Churchill, Atlee,

All heroes wield swords:

We are the sword.

Tom Stevens

Todmorden Market Close On A Saturday Afternoon

Four o'clock, four o'clock!
A small key entering the lock.
Count all the cash you got,
Shopping Shabbat comes to Tod.

Four o'clock, four o'clock!
Little crazy barking dog
Running in-between the stalls
Bringing trading to a close.

Four o'clock, four o'clock!
Boot doors of the vans go 'knock'.
Loaded trolleys everywhere -
Pensioners and dog beware!

Four o'clock, four o'clock!
Tower clock is saying tick-tock,
Wedding bells are saying ding-dong,
They will ring for very long.

Tick-tock, tick-tock,
Raindrops from the bridge go 'plock'.
And the Calder's ducks just might
Now enjoy a quiet night.

Oxana Poberejnaia

London And I

I love you in a way
That is hard to explain;
For you define parts of me
That is a mix of pain and gain.
You also tire me
From time to time;
And yet, you're always there
To clean me of my grime.
You enrapture me,
You capture me
And you catch me unawares;
For you are a city
That's forever in people's stares.
Your heart teams with people
And cultures galore;
With buses, trains and the mighty Tube -
Could I ever ask for more?
You reach out and welcome
Strangers old and new;
For you are London and I'm your child
And honour each other we do!

Sudakshina Bhattacharjee

A Great Place To Live

Bear no fear,
Better times are near.
A global recession,
Hard times in a recession,
Will all but be forgotten.
When we're on the up and no longer downtrodden.
Hard times will be forgotten.
As a fallen tree bears no fruit,
Time will pass,
Hardships will soon be forgotten.
The future is bright,
For each and every one of us.
Be positive.
Be well.
Better times are here again,
And that must never be forgotten.
The British Empire, will never be downtrodden.
The greatest empire this world has ever seen,
The strongest moral fibre,
Radiates from within.
The stiff upper lip,
The strength to carry on.
Bear no fear,
Good times will soon be here.

Darren P Morrall

These Things Remind Me Of You

Big Ben
Bowler-hatted men
Radio 4
Brighton beach shore
Ice cream cones
Garden gnomes
These things remind me of you.

Petticoat Lane
Summer days in the rain
The Gherkin
Birds chirping
Scones, jam and cream
Thinking of my football team
These things remind me of you.

Castle and lakes
Victoria sponge cakes
Counties and shires
Punting boats for hire
Telecom Tower
Houses of Parliament: seat of power
These things remind me of you.

Roses and daffodils
Lush, green grass and rolling hills
Picnics in the park
The sound of the lark
Cups of tea any time of the day
What more can I say?
These things remind me of you.

Mel Evans

Old Man Tay

Grey today
making his way
sluggishly, snailishly
trailing and oozing
till the tide turns, no running away
and what does he say,
old man Tay?

Yesterday
he was all for play
silver blue sparkles
chatter and gurgle
chasing and racing to fill up the sea.
Spring on the way
for old man Tay.

Lazy haze
of summer days
boating, fishing
counting the swans
taking for granted the birds and the bees
and timelessness
of old man Tay.

Calm and serene
till – splitting the scene
heron goes crashing
and flapping to launch
off the jetty and heavily labour upstream.
Wake from your dream
old man Tay!

Fecund and generous my silver-bright harvest,
fertile and fruitful my bank and my carse.
Bringer of life to all who come near me.
Kindly, benevolent old man? Why, of course.

Yet under that guise he is hiding a horror
with fingers of death and a curl of his lip.
Be wary; be sailors. No leeway for error.
Don't gamble on beating his stranglehold grip.

Will Wallace apart, (who was 'eight feet in stature'
and 'swam in full armour from shore unto shore')
how many men since, by chance or by anguish,
have gone without purpose beyond his dark door?

Now osprey dips in, unscathed, making circles
on silky smooth surface, seductive and sweet,
and dragonfly hangs, where all time seems suspended -
and memories of bodies devoured seem remote.

And on he goes
goes with the flow
never a worry
never says sorry.
He tells the timeless truth, yet lies
betrays without a qualm
then on a whim
gives up his prey
that he swept away.

What says he today,
old grey man Tay?
Mottled with granite as icy winds blow
and whip up the surface, reflecting the snow-
laden clouds, the ominous signs in the sky,
that angrily, bleakly, ask, 'Why?'
But will he reply?

Nesta Nicholson

Invitation From A Veteran

From battleground a voice called forth:
a weary tone which would escape
sourness of a drastic past
and a fragile present.

Bilateral contempt and worse
spat limpets who would not forsake
sourness of a drastic past
and a fragile present.

Slap intertidal of brave feet
fresh from the desiccated sands:
sourness of a drastic past
and a fragile present.

To build a future more complete,
though Noble went to doubtful hands:
sourness of a drastic past
and a fragile present.

From famous lough, shanty of peace
now resonates on tailored bridge,
rejoicing in the sweet release
from bitterness we chose to ditch.

No longer the malign refrain
as Derry welcomes with both arms
the absence of that stale old pain;
unshackled now its innate charms.

As echo from post-WWII,
North Ireland's bloom is calling you.
Walled city's hand now stretches forth . . .
Walled city's hand now stretches forth . . .

Perry McDaid

Kelvingrove Museum, Glasgow

There's a queue for Rembrandt's *Man in Armour.*
We wait, shuffle forward, earn our time in front.
Finally we stand exposed before a dark canvas
that's glossy as glass, sombre as sorrow.

A face emerges from the past, living, eternal
(though its owner has long been dry dust).
Colours bloom like flowers of night as crow-wing
shadows dominate the grave masterwork.

We long to be drawn further in, but the queue
coils behind us like a cortege. We move away,
glancing back at the creation that has confronted
us with death and sadness and time.

Now for the Impressionists, or the Glasgow Boys
or perhaps our much-loved Dali. For this
treasury is 'Scotland's', the city's, its people's.
It's ours – riches for free, yet priceless.

David McVey

My Isle Of Skye Girl

The hills seem endless,
Stitched with endless seams of green.
We sit together, hands entwined, and
Think of all that we have seen.
The fields have now turned golden,
The nights grow darker still.
I have loved you since the day we met,
Always have, always will.

Erica Kirk

England

Oh England how I miss you,
Now that you are far away.
All the things you have to offer,
I could cherish more each day.

To have a pint of ale,
In some quaint old country pub.
To see the Yorkshire Moors,
How I only wish I could.

To check the Pools and horses,
And have my modest fling.
To see the hopping robin,
Or hear a skylark sing.

To see the lights of Blackpool,
Or sail 'round Scarborough Bay.
To have to walk home from work,
On a cold and foggy day.

To see a coal fire burning,
On a cold and wintry night.
To read the daily papers,
Of the country's latest plight.

To see the sights of London
And bustle with the crowd.
To hear the different dialects
Of a nation old and proud.

These things I took for granted,
Now I miss each one in turn.
But I'll cherish them more dearly,
When to you England I return.

John Hopkins

Where The Rivers Meet (Kilsyth)

Where the rivers meet the ground is boggy
And wild flowers grow amid the sod
At the foot of the hills a little town grew
Where warriors fought since time began
Forts and walls snaked the land
Saints passed through in medieval train.

Where the rivers meet a battle was fought
As brother fought brother in civil war
For a religion that said, do not kill.
Splits in families swallowed like bitter pill
Ghosts in the nights may rise still
Over the bogs where cannon blew.

Where the rivers meet ruins stand silent
Looking over the town for a thousand years
Shadowed behind hills like a protective wall
Keeping safe the valley down below
The rivers meet at Caledonia's centre
In the valley rich and abundant.

Where the rivers meet in the valley quiet
The lands of Livingstone and Lennox
Along with the bell and book
Where weaving wove into history
And Garrel and Ebroch became as one
Flowing through the town of Kilsyth.

Andrew Provan McIntyre

South Molton

It used to be a fuzzy down
Now it is a market town
Gateway to Exmoor National Park
South Molton is renowned
The farmers plough in their fields
And they grow a lot of crops
Then they take them to the market
and some to the local shops
There is an annual sheep fair
an old tradition of years ago
The farmers take along their sheep
And look forward to some 'dough'
There is the old English fayre
And people dance in the square
Another old tradition
And everyone will be there
There is a very lovely church
Which is very near the square
And on a Sunday morning
People go to say a prayer
There are pubs that you can go to
If you want a gin and lime
And a clock is on the town hall
If you want to see the time!

We will now go to Exmoor
To see the panoramic view
And all the lovely wildlife
That Mother Nature knew
Wild ponies all around the moor
Where it is full of purple heather
And also with the yellow gorse
It all blends well together
The deer are a great attraction
And very much admired
And with foxes playing on the hills
I am sure you will be inspired.

So bring your friends to Exmoor
Let them feel the bracing air
And to enjoy the tranquillity
All the time that they are there.

Joan Herniman

Fenland Sunset

Spherical burnt orange hung over
the flat escarpment of day.
Cold, silvery and grey fish-like particles
fragmented the lake below,
Drifting sporadically like feathers
rippling against the water's edge.
Daylight disappeared slowly like a
thief in the night.
Its residual legacy resounding into
a fanciful flight of colour, texture and hue.
Woven into a thick velvety tapestry
rationed only by darkness;
Nature coloured my eyes as this
burning blaze of colour
Sunk deeper into the horizon
towards the close of day.
The giant saucer-like sunset
descended quickly into oblivion.

Christine Flowers

Yesterday

Walking along the towpath
Of Richmond long ago, seeing
Swans gliding on the River Thames.
To alight a boat for a trip to Hampton Court
A palace in a maze of history that grips the mind.
Another day to walk with big brother
To Kew Gardens. For a penny you could
Spend the day watching for birds to feed
Crumbs from your hand. Then play among
The lines of trees to the pagoda,
Till home time.
The boat race ended at Chiswick Bridge
Just a mile from where I lived. To buy
A light or dark blue flag we wave
These memories are in my mind like
Yesterday. A place once home seems
Many years ago.

Joyce Gale

England's Great Throne

Beyond this England's great throne I see
A picture of what used to be.
A sword enthroned to make a brave knight stand
Like a mighty musket from a Roundhead's hand.
The shroud that made the miller fall.
A land divided by Cromwell's sword.
This mighty island of hope and dreams,
Renew my boundless spirit to be set free.
I see my destiny anew
Of this, England's green and wondrous hue.
A sword will strike a valiant heart,
Let England cry
How great thou art.

Richard Charles

Aberfan

In Aberfan they played and sang
Dwarfed in the shadow of that satanic hill
Stopped in flight as the school bell rang
The sound of innocence would soon be still.
The groaning rumble of earth's black spew
Down that hillside slid
Faint barrier of gorse and bracken through
Havoc its destiny, infamy its bid.
No more laughter now, no song
Only darkness and dread abound
Man and nature's craven deed is done
The eerie silence of the lambs profound.
Posterity and bloodline now vanquished
No more children's children, no generations to come
Demised to the sessions of time
By the malevolent hand of man in a sea of scum.
What of you now, my beloved Aberfan, how do you mourn
I hold you dear in my bosom from across the ocean
I feel your intimate pain, your loss of first born,
Time is your only salvation.
There is no elixir, no magic potion.
In the Valleys they still lament your sadness Aberfan,
Testament to that fateful morning as the school bell rang.
In church and chapel, steeped in verdant Welsh hills
The choirs echo your sad refrain
As Mother Nature nestles in the twilight of stills.
Your memory will never wane Aberfan
In the gentle hush of morning, or at day's end
In the eclipse of the sun,
In constant as the ebb and flow of tide,
You will be there always Aberfan
Forever at my side.

Thomas Howard Jones

The English Nation

The Irish love the shamrock green
And Scotland sports the thistle blue,
In Wales daffodils and leeks are seen,
But the English emblem is the red rose true.

Red is the colour of the English blood,
Strong and bold as in days of yore.
Together we fight for what is right and good,
Supporting all inhabitants, rich and poor.

For we are folk of English birth,
From Celts and Saxons, Normans and Danes,
Immigrants from countries all over the Earth,
Bonded together in freedom, not chains.

A varied heritage we defend
And share our valued traditions here.
Over the years our many cultures blend
And this English nation is what we hold dear.

So on the 23rd of April
Let us join together with brave St George
To shout three cheers for the English nation
And vow that unity and love we'll forge.

Doreen Lawrence

Hinckley Town

Where do you live, I was once asked,
The town of Hinckley, which has quite a past.

Famous for the hosiery trade,
Where tights and stockings were once made.

'Argents Mead' and the memorial too,
Where we remember war veterans old and new.

Monday and Saturday is market day,
Where we all hope to get a bargain for the price we pay.

'Britannia Centre', well you should come and see,
With shops and a café, it's the place to be.

If you're feeling energetic and want to get fit,
Then the Leisure Centre is the important bit.

Food and drink we do not lack,
With many a bar just right for a snack.

You'll always find plenty of flowers around,
With baskets and tubs trailing to the ground.

There's a bus station, train station
And we're near the motorway,

So why not come over and spend a great day.

Alain Sequeira

Verses To Please Round Our Norton Lees

Take trip down Memory Lane and drift into the Past,
Hear the sound of lowing cattle, milking time at last.
Wander through the fields and farm-lands, how it used to be.
Take a walk near Meersbrook House, the peacocks you will see.

Make your way towards the woods and paddle in the stream.
Climb the hill and cross the field, dogs barking it would seem,
Further on there stands a building looking fine and tall,
Then as you move in closer, you will see the name 'Lees Hall'.

Sit down by the duck pond on this gorgeous day.
Watch the horses pull the plough, when they pass by this way.
Listen to the birdsong, high up in the trees,
Savour smells of baking bread, drifting on the breeze.

Up you go through Cockshutts Farm, then across the lane,
Travel past the Hollies, Lees House, then back again.
West House on your left, Mullberry Cottage at the end,
Make your way to 'Bishops House' it's just around the bend.

See the ancient pottery, on the sloping shelf,
Jugs and bowls and dishes, seem to hold on by themselves.
I'm sure they must be stuck in place, to stay put for so long,
Or someone could remove them, and that would be quite wrong.

Should you have an inclination or ability,
Dreaming all your days away in sweet tranquillity,
With the scent of honeysuckle, roses round your door,
The lark in the air and sunshine, would you need much more.

When the happy day is over, and the sun sinks in the west,
Birds and beasts and creatures, they settle down to rest.
Owls begin their hooting and you'll hear the vixen cry.
Then you'll see the pale moon as she drifts across the sky.

Soon we're back from Memory Lane,
Could we livc back then again?
Midst the farmlands, fields and trees
How time has changed our Norton Lees.

Beryl Heathcote

Spring At Home In The Wyre Forest

I am truly blessed to live where I do,
I gaze out my window at the wondrous view.
Swathes of colour behold my eyes.
The forest looms under bright blue skies.
The Severn meanders sparkling in the sun.
Spring is born; new lives have begun.

Baby lambs frolic in the fresh green grass,
They nudge their mums as they wander past.
Birds gather at the feeders in their vast array
And fallow deer can be seen not very far away.
Pheasants vie with each other to claim their ground.
The sounds of nature can be heard all around.

A blue tit fledgling flutters, its mouth agape
Awaiting its parent perching on the gate.
Butterflies spread their wings to fly
Over colourful wild flowers riding high.
The song of the blackbird trilling in the trees.
The sound of buzzing nectar-hugging bees.

At the bottom of my garden a whistle sounds
As the Severn Valley train, along the track does bound.
Steam rising high, billowing up to the sky,
As the magnificent train goes chugging by.
From Kiddy to Bridgnorth it makes its way.
A picturesque journey to make on this sunny day.

Nature is so rewarding; a pleasure indeed,
How large ash trees grow from such small seeds.
How the seasons come and the seasons go,
I will always marvel at this magnificent show.
I found treasure in the beauty of my wonderful view
And I know I am amongst a privileged few.

Margaret Rosentritt

69

Tenby

In a small corner of South West Wales lies
A town that's a holiday resort
Though Tenby is small, it's crowded like flies
With people from all over Loke Alsalts

You have all you need, from pillar to post
Two long beaches, no beach parking space
Plenty of car parks, an island to coast
All should go there, it's a lovely place

Tenby is so popular, a friendly place
Everyone from England rushes down that way
Once you have been there, and sampled the taste
Of fresh clean waters, the breeze in your face.

In the summer, Tenby's rich in the money
Crowded with people, and crowded with fun
But in the winter, a ghost town not funny
There's no people about, no not one.

Margaret Burtenshaw-Haines

Stockport

S un shining on the precinct of
T he town that has many places
O f historical interest.
C hadkirk Trail and Bramhall Hall
K eep visitors coming.
P laza Theatre has a variety of shows
O f excellent performance.
R oman lakes add their own charm
T o this interesting town.

Diane Duff

True Blue

I'm patriotic to the core
No one loves their country more
Than me.
Proudly British through and through,
My colours are red, white and blue.
That's me.
I can't abide ex-patriots
Who live in distant foreign spots
And fret
About the way this country's run,
The frequent rain, and little sun
We get.
Let words of scorn pour from their lips,
Greased by continental chips
And drink.
May they remain on foreign shores,
We're better off without these bores
I think.

Ron Missellbrook

My City And Me

We can listen to a million languages
My city and me,
Or let the sound wash over us
Like waves in a warm sea.

C A Mackie

Ties That Bind . . .

Once the warm summer breeze kissed a broad open field
that swept down to the old farm-lane . . .
I close my eyes for a moment,
and I see it all again.

The school nestling next to the chapel
the worn steps leading up to the door . . .
the children with hoops and marbles
and the chanting of four-times-four.

And here's Grandpa's forge on this corner,
I peep in and he's working inside . . .
I hear the clang of his hammer,
see the sparks flying up to the sky.

Here's the old village shop that my grandmother owned . . .
as she walked she'd jangle her keys!
There's a hole in the counter to drop money through,
and a good smell of bacon and cheese.

The lovely old farmyard would fill with the bustle
of milking, or carting the hay.
Now it's silent and grim, and the rain drips in,
and the white walls are dingy and grey.

Once the hub of the village it held pride of place,
now deserted and ruined, but few
care a jot for the farm with its sagging front door,
and the roof with its ribs poking through.

High up on the moor, 'neath the brambles and nettles
are stones, where a cottage once stood:
no neighbours around, just the blue distant sea,
and the singing of birds in the wood.

Here Mum and Dad lived, and my sister was born,
and many are the tales I've heard tell
how coal came by cart, and the water was brought
through the woods, from a little old well.

But the years have rolled by, many old things have gone . . .
modern buildings have taken their place . . .
but memories remain of simpler days
when life moved at a gentler pace.

Though I've travelled abroad, and gazed in awe
at the wonders of Planet Earth,
precious memories of home keep calling me back
to Wales . . . and this place of my birth.

Audrey Moore

The Beneficence Of Rain

Liquid pattering in the rain-soaked wood,
A mystic, green and watery world.
Tiny, creeping plants and towering trees
All gladly drinking-in the downpour's blessing.
Never despise our English rain,
Creator of this lush and verdant land,
Preserver of our lakes, and trees
Which stand graceful and proud for centuries.
The seasons roll along in endless beauty,
Daffodil bright in pale Spring sunshine,
Hazy in Summer's heat, buzzing with bees,
The burnished, coppery glow of Autumn
Fading to Winter's stark silhouettes
With seagulls shrieking over cold, grey seas.
This northern land was born to rain,
Our drenching showers make it grow and thrive,
Resonant with birdsong, rich in plants – alive!
The moist and fertile soil of England's far North West
Must, surely, rank amongst the country's best.

Ann Warren

Thruxton

I love this little village
It's full of style and grace
I love this little village
It's just in the right place.

Every bend and corner
Waits for one and all
A gardening club and WI
In the memorial hall.

The roads are clean and tidy
The hedges trimmed right back
There is a park for everyone
And a racing track.

The church stands mostly silent
Till someone rings the bell
The walls are steeped in history
As historians will tell.

Allotments stand on Roman's past
Filled with fruits and fair
For birds it is a haven
Also for fox and hare.

This village is so tiny
Yet we have a landing plot
Emergency, emergency we have got the lot
It is a lovely spot.

So green it's like an emerald
Full of little gems
With lots of pretty colours
Hanging from tall stems.

We have a little brook
That wanders through it all
A little trundling bus
And a postman comes to call.

There is a little school
With lots of little tots
Their schooling is quite excellent
Varying lots and lots.

Horses tread the village
But they're not on parade
Just exercising fetlocks
Whilst the riders hold the reins.

All in all it is a merry song
In this tiny village
The place where I belong
Where people like to throng.

Hidden in Old Hampshire
Not far from the sea
Thruxton is my village
You are welcome, come and see.

Janet Vessey

Borders

Here among herbaceous borders
Lie the dreams of Englishmen
A plot of land, some bricks, some mortar
And the will to get by, best we can
That is what our people do
And have done for long centuries past
We are sanctuary for those who suffer
And reach our safer shores at last
Our land has seen many battles
Fought tyrants from afar and near
We've spilled blood and mourned our kinsmen
In the fight for the land which we hold dear
We have faced long trials and hardships
And, no doubt will do again
For here among herbaceous borders
Lie the dreams of Englishmen.

Marji Tomlinson

The Isle Of Sheppey

The Isle of Sheppey is famously peppy -
The air there is second to none.
And the islanders boast that, on parts of their coast,
If you're lucky, you may glimpse the sun.

The Isle is unmatched, being semi-detached
From the mainland because of The Swale -
A sort of deep ditch, the bridge over which
Some may think is a bit out of scale.

As a tourist resort you might think Sheppey ought
To deserve a much wider acclaim
From holidaymakers and mini-break takers,
But it doesn't, and that is a shame.

There are chances for larks in the caravan parks,
And, of course, Leysdown's quite celebrated
For its 'Kiss-Me-Quick' hats, and a late-night life that's
Pretty generally under-rated.

Some parts of the Isle, every once in a while,
Are awash when the sea is in flood,
And a walk on its beaches is something that teaches
The meaning of 'stick-in-the-mud'.

But still, there are some who have just had to come
And enjoy Sheppey's charms at their leisure:
Their good conduct reward is a spell of free board
On the Isle Her Majesty's pleasure.

Queenborough's calm has its own kind of charm,
And, like Minster, is very historic.
And Eastchurch is where men first took to the air,
Although how they did that defies logic.

There will be rather less of the port of Sheerness
If doom-laden forecasts are right,
And explosives galore in a wrecked ship off-shore
One day blow up, as some say that they might.

The flora and fauna that lurks in this corner
Of Kent, is a joy to behold,
But you won't have to mind if what you'd hoped to find
Has found somewhere less bitterly cold.

Sheppey's no South Sea isle, but it has its own style,
With which local folk are content.
They're quite happy to be on what mainlanders see
As a slightly odd outpost of Kent.

Alan Bignell

Victorious Memories

Here we step into this gracious land, triumphant sounds abound,
The brass band plays as our British summer sun puts on another grand display.
A cold silky 99 cornet, families laughing, water splashing,
And our clever bumblebee, all wonderful memories for me.

The rolling hills blend and curve protecting us against the enemy as we served.
Buried in our fertile soul, men, fathers, husbands and brothers,
Leaving their loved ones – some so young, and leaving their mothers,
Loyal to this land, for our freedom.

This day we share in happiness not fear,
We remember all those we hold dear,
We're asked not now to shed a tear.

Instead to smile and look forward to clear skies – the clouds part for the sun,
The sunken ships foregone, in the midst.
Life returns in memories of fun,
It's here now, on this wondrous kissed grass – we won.

Victorious, standing tall and proud to our feet,
We stand together, no defeat.
Placing our hand on our heart, singing joyously loud that we are a part,
Of this fanfare – this celebration of life,
To which we commit our body, mind and light.

Emma Lannigan

The Place I Call Home

Let me take you on a journey
Of the place I call my home.
Let me give you little snapshots.
Through my Highlands let us roam.

Majestic and ancient, defining the land
Are the Scottish Highland mountains.
When sunshine melts the covering snow,
Little streams jump over stones – nature's fountains.

The rivers swell – the salmon leap,
Like silver are lochs and streams.
Winter's might now gone, new life appears,
As nature awakes from its dreams.

Gold covers the land, flowering rape and broom
Reflecting the rays of the sun.
Deep green of the trees is framing the gold,
A sign that spring has won.

Forests are alive with birds and deer,
Ewes with their lambs populate meadows.
Cows proudly watch their little calves,
Then settling down under evening shadows.

Seagulls will wake you to a new day,
Be it sun, be it rain, or haar.
Weather changes the scenery, what yesterday
Looked so near, today seems so far.

Seasons soon change, the harvest gathered in,
And autumn winds are sweeping the land;
Greens changing to brown, nights turning cold,
Great waves are covering white sand.

Migrating birds are filling the sky.
Fruits hang heavy on branches.
So plentiful are the blessings for all,
We celebrate with Ceilidhs and dances.

And not to be forgotten a most beautiful sight,
Like gossamer curtains in the night,
Delicate colours, not too bright,
A playful sky – what a delight!
Have you ever seen the Northern Light?

My Scottish Highlands – my home!

Helga Dharmpaul

Watching The World Go By

Cars, motorcycles, tall buildings,
Noise, traffic, people,
Running, walking, shouting,
Then . . .
The whole world became a microscopic image of beauty.

Tall buildings, small buildings,
Unusual individuals, plain individuals.
Each with a story to tell . . .
Each with an identity
So as I am sitting here,
Moving at a fast pace . . .
Trees, sun, sky, the glimmer of tranquillity – I realise that beyond the grass,
The fields, the trees . . .
Despite absorbing nature faster than Man itself,
Moving at this fast pace

Britain really is . . .
The most wonderful place.

Helen Searle

A View Of The Black Country

A coal seam runs across South Staffordshire
Known to the Romans and 30 feet thick;
Where miners descend, our 'into the thick'
And fumes are hurled up into the atmosphere.
Only in Brierley Hill is the air clear,
Coal-fired furnaces pumping out flames:
Noxious air, slag heaps, this Hell has a name,
Reborn 'the Black Country' and without peer.

The earth pockmarked where industry has been,
A network of canals are the highway
For the Black Country, in these glory days.
Vegetation succumbed, no fields of green,
Widespread devastation, no shrubs are seen.
An image of Hell across the coal field,
Black diamonds and gold the coal seam does yield,
Not pastoral idylls with waters clean.

Embraced under a darkened canopy,
Hard graft now in an industrial age;
World renown, the Black Country's heritage,
Black as the coal dug from the collieries.
Locks, boiling cauldrons, tubes and foundries,
Geological minerals the backbone:
Iron-making based on coal and limestone,
Development of heavy industry.

Disembowelled earth is seen for miles around
Out of the coal mines the black gold is won,
A constant cloud of smoke blocks out the sun.
The landscape is broken by cinder mounds,
Furnace refuse where iron ore is bound
And then being run out into the pig beds,
The smelting process from the funnel heads
And ore, coal and limestone from underground.

Nothing by day but burning furnaces
And mountains of cinder and earth laid bare;
Manufacturing at night under glare
Of lurid smoke-stacks and dirty faces.
Day and night the same under the surface
For men of iron harvesting the coal

In mineshafts, 'in the thick', deep in their holes:
Calloused hands, backs bent and far from God's grace.

Air pollution confuses day and night
For those in workshops and down the coal pits;
Dudley's chains and Walsall's bridle bits,
Wolverhampton's locks made by candlelight.
Anchors and cables forged by Cradley's might,
Oldbury's saucepans, rivets, bolts and nuts;
Wednesbury's tubes on the banks of the cut,
Black Country's industrial dreams burn bright.

Ian Henery

Lincolnshire

On the sunrise ridge where Norsemen strode
And legions gazed I watch the unfurl
Of sky unlimited as through the corntide
Giants walk unbowed by Heaven.

From fishroad to eelslide river,
Guided by quaking alder spires,
The clockmakers of the universe
Rebuilt the world from a violet's leaf.

Bishop and poets called it home.
Moonsteps beyond the man-shaped fen
Released God's words to soar and then
Poachers and ploughmen made it home.

This belly of England, carved from wold chalk
By butterfly blue wings, unfolds
Beneath me in a mist of green and sky,
Broader than a poet's dream, crowds heaven around us.

Howard Hewson

Thrills And Spills On Cooper's Hill

It started many years ago,
The reason no one seems to know,
Like some ancient mystic rhyme,
Whose origins are lost in time.

The annual pilgrimage takes place,
to witness an astonishing race.
Thousands flock here every year,
to Cooper's Hill in Gloucestershire.

Competitors are all in line,
and gaze down at the steep incline.
Some faces showing signs of fear,
They ask, 'What am I doing here?'

No time for doubt or change of heart,
The race is now about to start.
A Double Gloucester rolls down the hill,
and signals time for thrills and spills.

'They're off' to chase the rolling cheese,
Many tumble grazing arms and knees,
Careering down the deep descent,
The crowd roar on encouragement.

Slipping, sliding, moans and groans,
Somersaults and broken bones,
Medics standing by to ease,
the self-inflicted injuries.

Each race is roared on loud and clear,
The winners get a healthy cheer.
They grab the special hard-earned prize,
Held up in triumph to the skies.

The rest trudge off, they all came near,
Perhaps some will come back next year.
For then the droves will come again,
no matter if it's sun or rain.

As for me, I never will,
Chase a cheese down Cooper's Hill.
If I want a cheese I'll gladly pay,
It's so much easier that way!

Stephen Oxlee

Amazingstoke

My British town
Makes me proud
It's full of cups of tea
In my house in Oakridge
By the huge oak tree

Take a stroll down the road
So many dogs go by
Go shopping in The Malls
In the south, see the food festivals

See the St George's Cross fly high
Pop into the pub for a pint
By the fields of yellow corn
It's such a delightful sight

The Olympic torch went by
The War Memorial Park with Basingstoke Live
The Holy Ghost Chapel Mrs Blunden buried alive
See the history in the museum survive

This town is full of talent
Steve Hewlett from Britain's Got Talent
A three-legged dog Haatchi with Little B
Talented performers, theatres, there's so much to see.

Lucy Lincoln

A Great Land's Tale

This is the tale
Of a wonderful land
Of mighty kingdom
And the royals so grand

The glorious aura!
Straight away it is felt
By the bricks and buildings
Its immensely rich history is being spelt

For good or may be not quite so
It is up to you to decide
But some valuable legacies were sure left
From the days when its rule spread far and wide

It is a hub of knowledge
And exciting discoveries
The world-renowned
Are its prestigious schools and universities

From beautiful green countrysides
To the mountains, streams and rivers
From surprising by its varied terrain
That small island does not fail to deliver

Admittedly enough
It seems to get more than its fair share of rain
But with all these great museums and galleries for indoors
There is no excuse to sit in vain

On that island
The life is enriched with cultural diversity
You get hooked
To its engaging versatility

This is the strategy
The majority there deems worthy to implement
Because through their variations
Each other they inspire and complement

Ahead of the nation of course
Are ever new trials
But they will hopefully be overcome
By its people with innovative styles

I hope that you have enjoyed
This simple but deep tale
You sure would have guessed the place
For I have been leaving a clue-laden trail

Compared to my fellow writers and poets
I have got nothing to show off
But I just feel honoured
To contribute to this Great British Write Off

So dear reader!
If so, be proud to be British
You can aspire to be whatever you dream of
In this fact let yourself relish

Or . . .
With so much to discover and do
There is no room for boredom
And if you haven't yet done so
You better pay a visit to the United Kingdom!

Javeria A Sarfraz

Bradwell

When I think of a village, I see a village green, with quaint olde worlde houses in a row
There's a tavern on the corner where the old men sit and dream,
And spin yarns of what they did so long ago.
You don't go the bakers just to buy a crusty loaf
Or a batch of fresh baked scones so hot and new
Because the lady round the counter likes to have a friendly chat
And takes an interest in everything you do.
There's a funny little post office with a bell above the door
Which smells a lot of paraffin and soap
And there's a shelf up in the corner with all different sorts of sweets
And boxes full of nails and coils of rope.
The boy scouts have a jumble sale inside the village hall,
And mums and grans all help and make the tea
And anyone and everyone always has a stall,
And everyone's as happy as can be.
The gardening club put on a show, the competition's high,
The trophy is on everybody's minds,
There's chutneys, jams and cakes and scones,
So much to feed the eye and vegetables of every single kind.
Everyone goes carolling when all the world is white,
And hot punch handed thankfully around,
And the little church on Christmas Eve is filled to overflow
And love and friendship really do abound.
Now Bradwell may not be quite the village of my dreams,
But some of it's the same you will agree
And I get a funny feeling that however far I roam,
Bradwell is still waiting there for me.

Jo Graystone

This Little Town

This little town has many twinned lives,
A town, a village, a hamlet,
A parade, a fete, a fair,
The Queen's coronation and jubilee all celebrated through the generations
with reminiscence and a cream tea.
The boards of our little theatre have been graced with Charlie Chaplin.
Church green has welcomed many a young lover's first stroll or last tearful
embrace.
Young women assembled needles in the factories young men shared their last
prayer
in St Stephen's Church before marching off to war.
Little Arrow Brook still flows on a peaceful summer's evening
curving where Roman soldiers took a rest on the riverbank.
Along the same riverbank where Sistine monks walked up from Boardsley
Abbey
overlooked by the red north sky.
This little town is like its emblem the little kingfisher,
it dives and rises to reveal its beautiful array of colours.

Natalie Brookes

Teignmouth Promenade

The storms we had this winter turned our lovely promenade into a war zone.
We had to wait a long time as the engineers were busy on the hanging
Dawlish railway line.
A feat of engineering to be seen to be believed
Flowerbeds have been rebuilt and plants begin to grow
And now we're waiting for our pier to open once again.
Nearly washed away
But when it's done, another faits accomplis
And our little town will be restored to loveliness once more,
The sea will not defeat us, we are back to beauty as before.

Caroline Garland Adams

What 'Er You See

I do not wish to travel
to wild and far-off places
here upon St Leonards beach
are happy, smiling faces,
fish and chips to die for!
Huge seagulls ride the breeze
the Old Town is, the place to be
'Go on, buy all you please.'

The lazy days of summer
give way to autumn's air
evening light is passing by
morning dew is fresh and fair,
I love what life bestows
winter's always fun for me
I see the lights, of
Charlotte's cottage
where Yuletide cider flows.

Church bells signal Christmas
in a twilight crisp and cold
over the valley, in
castles dark
pipers don't grow old,
a distant field with mighty oaks
looks free of trampled snow
not for long, I've noticed
it's where the ramblers go.

What I love about my house
is living beneath the thatch
'Don't be shy, when passing by
come on in and lift the latch,
I'll tell you of its history
and how it came to be
it's thirsty work, make no mistake
we'll make some time for tea.'

Out beyond the graveyard
is where I think the most
even get to chat awhile
with a witty, handsome ghost!

We both agree together
that England is our home, and
that when, the Romans visited
they soon went back to Rome.

Marie Marshal

The British Isles

A country of great contrasts
Scotland renowned for her stunning scenery
Green-scented pine forests, heather-clad glens
Her winding rivers gurgling over rocks, luminary
Waterfalls tumbling down hillsides, cascading,
Spilling onto beautiful rocky coves, their white sands
Bathed in sea spray where seagulls soaring, wielding
Overhead, then landing precipitously on pounding waves
Or balancing on ragged rocks. Scotland, where my
Ancestors have lived since 1200, in a land of castles,
History and dreams, a beautiful corner of the Kingdom
A naturally formed, wild nature reserve.

The British Isles with many varied and beautiful areas
Throughout the Kingdom to settle, explore. Firstly, and
Importantly, England is a multicultural society.
A place to reside without fear, as a free person.
Living in a democracy, a land of opportunities,
Where help and advice are available for each person.
Free healthcare, for those requiring treatments.
A land where everyone has the opportunity to learn,
Earn and build a future for themselves, their families.
Everything you need is here, your expectations can be
Realised, by your own actions.
'Je pense plus' I think much, our family motto.

Erskine

What Is It?

It isn't the glorious coastline, lovely though it be
From the singing sands of Bamburgh to the Tyne on the cold North Sea
Nor is it the sacred peace of Lindisfarne, famed over all the earth
As the cradle of Christianity in this noble land of my birth
Neither is it the rolling Cheviot hills or Simonside's lofty dome
Ever calling to sons and daughters: Why don't you come back home?
Even the mighty Roman Wall cannot sum up its appeal
So just what is it about this land that earthly senses cannot reveal?

It's surely the Northumbrian people themselves that hold the secret's key
As sturdy and trusty as those ancient hills beside that cold North Sea
Shaped as they are by history's hand and the message of saints of old
They're worthy successors in time to yesterday's knights so bold
Dancing to music that's come down through the years with its own distinctive sound
And talking a dialect known only to them who were born of this piece of ground
Long may they last like the land they love
And the future their faithful legacy prove.

Meg Gilholm

Magnificent Great Britain

A country of pride
A union of cultures
A voice of freedom
A passion of diversity
A right of way
Justice, equality, peace
A view of excellence
A way of life
A drive to succeed
A combination of backgrounds
It is most definitely a
United Kingdom!

Sobina Mahboob

Dawlish Water

At the end of our garden there runs forever a stream.
In summer a soft and delicate background splashing
Enhances my dreams;
In winter a windswept torrent from the moor
Runs down,
Between the steep-sided cleft,
A mere ten yards or so from my back door.
One long ago, rain-drenched October it broke its banks,
Intruding into the garden itself,
Until the weather calmed, and the level sank once more.
This year, so little rain fell, the stream was almost stilled,
But then the drought broke; once again the night was filled
With the ever-moving, narcotic heartbeat of the stream
Pulsing its way towards the sea, the self-fulfilling dream
Of all rivulets, rivers, streams, burns and rills,
Themselves in ever-perpetual motion
Till time itself is stilled.
My element is fire,
But I have a strong affinity with water.
Fire gives heat and warms the bones,
But only water has the gift of laughter . . .
In a contented well-filled mood, it bubbles and burbles
Over stones, as a full-fed babe chatters and gurgles
Delightedly; imbuing the watcher and the listener
With a sense of quiet peace,
As it moves ever onward and forward,
Yet forever filling the space it leaves . . .
And so my stream exists,
Dying and living contemporaneously,
Laughing at life, and laughing at death . . .

Jenny Proom

Sydenham

I've lived in Sydenham nearly 94 years
Born in a house five minutes away.
I've seen many changes in the streets
Which had cobbled stones and trees.
In my early life our house was big,
With a garden which extended to woods.
We lost this one during World War Two
When the bombs fell, and we had to move.
Many other old buildings also went
And we had to find somewhere to live.
This one I moved into in 1946,
Which was damaged, but newly rebuilt,
Sydenham has certainly changed a lot.
None of the old shops are left,
The church, St Bartholomew's still remains,
Surrounded by gravestones with familiar names,
Of loved ones, who now have left,
Traffic roars up and down the roads,
And the trains stop at the station.
The railway lines were laid in the old canal,
And London is not far away,
So the village of Sydenham is no longer there,
But my memories still remain,
I hope God will let me carry on here
And not take me away just yet.

Doris Pullen

My Country

The land of song, my homeland, Creoso, glorious Wales
'Calon Lan' 'Myfanwy' are vocalised thru hills and vales
Rugged majestic mountains, many a stately castle exalted every one
Testament to years of battle, some lost but mostly won
The rills, the streams, the rivers, babbling, tumbling as they go
From mountain tops to valleys cascading, then meandering as on their way they flow
Past pit heads most now silent, black sentinels of yore
No miners' feet clatter the roadways home their lamps are lit no more
Pit ponies now out grazing, green meadows and warm sunshine to enjoy at last
The wooden pit props crumbling, their job done, long in the past.
Slag heads now are landscaped, nature's beauty reclaimed at cost
Miners no more breathe black dust, therefore, not all is lost
Our coastline quite outstanding, awesome cliffs, some sheer outcrops
Miles of sandy beaches, pretty harbours, colourfully yachts
Children happy building sandcastles, or jumping over some small waves
The bolder ones exploring rock pools, some grottos or deep caves
The daffodils, leeks, red dragon emblems most dear, each one,
Ancient history our heritage, many valiant deeds well done.

Marjorie Leyshon

These British Isles

These British Isles, my homeland, a heritage ancient and proud,
In palaces and cathedrals, we sing the praises loud.
Monuments of history we can recall, statues of heroes, we salute them all.
Loyalty from our men and women, brave deeds in troubled years,
Defended from aggressors to live in peace, and dispel all fears.
An emblem, the rose, a King's own choice, to bloom where'ere, as we rejoice.
The thistle, shamrock and daffodil,
To share our pride and hearts to fill.
God bless who rule over us in our multicultured land,
Grant succour to the settlers, hold out a friendly hand.
Descendents of our ancestors, loyal, noble and strong
Gave their lives for Britain, we praise them loud and long.
In our beloved country with green and fertile lands
We see the beauty that surrounds us, made by God's own hands.
Sparkling lakes and rivers, a pleasure to us all
Designed flora and fauna, answers every call.
Glorious endeavours of the past with a history sublime,
Traditions of these British Isles, this homeland of mine.

Patricia Evans

Beautiful Kent

I have travelled throughout Britain, and wherever I went
I always thought 'beautiful', but not quite like my Kent
Here, in Northfleet, that's where I live, it's a beautiful scene
Wherever one looks, they are surrounded by green
Green fields, green gardens and lovely green trees
Which are filled with beautiful birds, butterflies and humming bees
The neighbours are kind on the estate where I live
And if anyone needs help, they are always willing to give
We have our own church, shops and a pub with a family bar
And close by is a motorway with easy access by car
All my life I have lived here in Kent
And I can honestly say my life has been well spent.

Pat Maynard

Redcastle

Weeping red sandstone walls
Crying over past glories
Derelict towers still standing tall
Unable to narrate their lifetime stories

Empty window openings
Highlight an inner soul
Safe in the knowledge
That its former role
In Scotland's democracy will never
Be surpassed by any crumbling mediocrity

Now standing hidden in the trees
Gently swaying in the early morning breeze
This baronial splendour does not fret
Neither does it regret
Redcastle guards intimate secrets well
As it cannot speak or quietly tell

After eight hundred turbulent years
Shedding more than just a few tears
A shell that is still visually
Appealing to the eyes
Awaits its future or final sad demise.

Bill Wilson

London

Epping Forest, in London's Essex county
Is a brand new world, for me
I escape the rat race, and city lights
And have trees . . . for company.
The old London, Essex fog
Is a cloak of security,
And the autumn mist, an invisible kiss
Heals my insecurity.
Yeah London swings, it's a sixties' thing
With hippies, mods and rockers
Let's go down to London Town
And don't forget the workers and the dockers.
Meanwhile I lay in this forest
Beneath a starry sky
It's a magic night, and feels so right
I feel like I could fly.
I hear the faint sound, of busy traffic
Out there in the distance
It's morning time, and I feel just fine
Such is my existence.
Later on, I will make my way
Back to the open road
Watching commuters, rush to the station
So they can sit, and unload.
Not for me . . . this humdrum life
For others, it's a pity
But I'm laid-back, and I won't crack
Like stressed workers in the city.
Well I've said my piece . . . I have my peace
And I am at that stage
I'm gonna relax, forget council tax
I really should, at my age.
I love London, and always will
I will never stray too far.
London, is the heartbeat of life
It's here . . . it's now . . . it's where you are.

Dave Kwiatkowski

Who Do They Think They Are?

Many Hull people are aggrieved
At the way they feel that Hull's perceived
If Southern Softies are to be believed
Hull should never have been conceived.
Just who do they think they are?

We don't have Kew Gardens or the O2 Arena
St Paul's Cathedral or the tennis for Serena
But, there's more to us than chavs in trackies
Or burger and chips at Ronald Mackies.
Just who do they think we are?

We don't need posh shops to get our kicks
Like Harrods and Tiffany or Harvey Nicks
We've got Primark, Poundland and pick 'n' mix
And a late night pharmacy for a methadone fix.
Just who do they think we are?

Hull's heritage is strong and its people are tough
We can laugh at ourselves when the going gets rough
And now we're saying 'we've about had enough
Of the snipes and the digs from the 'not-know-enoughs'
Just who do they think they are?

So what makes us different, what makes us renown?
What makes Hull Yorkshire's jewel in the crown?
Well, we coped with the Blitz without going down
And the floods and recession with barely a frown.
So who do we think we are?

Well, we think we're quite special and caring and strong
We think our history says we belong
To a group far from the back of beyond
So who do they think they are?
Who are you? Who are you? Who r ya? Who r ya?

Catherine Scott

East Ender

I grew in the maze of the East by the Krays,
City lights and nightlife just a bus ride away,
The lane of bricks with fields that spit art and paint sprayed,
Backstreets where pavements meet the Bishops Gate.
The chapel they coloured white stood with market signs and fruits,
With the deepest roots like the beggar that was blind.
Been a Bethnal girl, a Stepney girl, the Cockney kind,
But Hackney was the birth of my Eastern times.
The hospital of mothers where Homerton found,
Babies of the East and jungle sounds.
No well in the street but on Well Street ground,
Stands an orchard with voices where a ring o' roses go around.
A child of the oldskool before the change began,
We dialled 533 after 0181.
The Hall in the town led us further out,
By the hop on buses and shish houses.
A journey at its best we grew where East kept,
Reels of pictures at the house until that field turn West.
The roads we stamped on where we grew as kids,
Now the face of the birth of the Olympics.
East is in my genes, Middle East of the Earth,
Home where sounds reach Bows from the church.
Footprints we made in concrete and wood,
Preserved our young whispers of childhood.
Eastern smiles we made at the Children's Museum
With laughter in tune like echoes of London Colosseum.
The life we lived in every block,
To the walk we made to the bagel shop,
The hands we looked for at the station clock,
To memories of the day at St Catherine's Dock.
The East in me created many nights of craft for escaping
Tears that The Thames waved in when bridges were breaking.
The walls we knew were set in stone,
And nothing beats this place called home.
An Easterner at heart this life was designated,
To come pass all the trials and tribulations,
I keep these memories to ever feel reinstated,
30 years East then I emigrated.

Nadia Fahmy

Orpington

Orpington is far from a wonderful place,
In fact, in some ways, I might say a disgrace,
Sometimes I feel I'm risking my fate,
Whenever I enter the Ramsden Estate,
The buildings are grey and pollution is rife,
But the people ensure it's a wonderful life.

The nature on show is next to none,
There isn't much round here to do for fun,
If you're looking for substance, style and grace,
I'll tell you right here, you're in the wrong place,
Even the gardens you can't call a park,
But the people round here are such a great lark!

There's Steven and Ashley and Thomas and Sam,
They are the people that make Orpington glam,
You can't forget Rachel and Emma and Kat,
You needn't look any further than that.
So don't look for perfection or you'll never be pleased,
Just remember these facts and you'll feel at ease.

Tom Fitton

A Great Big Move

To grow in decade deep in the south
Always reminded to rush about, from the worst place in London
Unto the greats of Westminster, just to end up back to a place unknown

To be raised in the north both far and wide
To be treated friendly as we know the Scottish has pride
To be treated as liar, a cheat, a scoundrel, just for the Scouse accent

To run away and still live nearby
To listen to the Welsh and Irish give good advice
To move so close and live far away
I say Cambridge has a brilliant smile today
But shall remain at home in the heart of hearts
Bedford it shall be for it has stole my love.

Rebecca Sellis

The Envy Of The World

With Celtic tribes and Romans
Who found this Island place
With Vikings and with Saxons
We formed the English race

With Normans and with others
Who came with us to stay
We forged the English language
And lived the English way

We laughed with English humour
When others scowled and cursed
And always England did its best
When others did their worst

We know that English freedoms
Were bought with English pain
And this example to the world
Forever will remain

When English airmen fought above
And English seamen fought below
When English soldiers fought alone
To once again defeat a foe

Our English fathers, brothers died
That English freedoms were not lost
Their heritage was England's past
To fight and not to count the cost

All countries know of England
To England we owe a debt
And all who made us what we are
We never can forget

So Englishmen can walk with pride
Because it flags unfurled
Wave on for hope and liberty
The envy of the world.

Robert Cairns Harrison

Homecoming

It's been a long and bloody war
Some comrades I have lost.
And looking back I ask myself
Why? And then what for?

The long, long days and eerie nights
I have been so alone
But now it's done, the plane's touched down
At last I am back home.

The cosy feel in the village pub
Where locals gather as a friendly club
Having a glass, sharing a joke
Here you are family, not just some bloke.

Wake in the morning to the song of the birds
Watch the farmer driving his herd.
With a sigh of contentment
Breathe in the fresh morning air
Dear old England, none can compare.

In this small sleepy village
No longer alone
This is sheer heaven
This is my home.

Audrey Allocca

Norfolk Has Blue Eyes

She don't cry easy, so much
of the rain
passing down
to the hills out west.

I've seen snow shower clouds
come and go
across them skies.

You catch names
that clash like bangles falling
up and down the maid's arms:
Hindolveston, Coltishall, Blickling, Wells

all summer long, stretching
long limbs out at Holkham,
jiving, lindy-hopping till all hours,
grass-wild poppied hair
flying tangled, salty. What can you do?

And when she jumps, strings
of small shells rattling at her breast:
Crostwick, Snettisham, Stalham, Holt,
trinkets in a net. Lovelier

than proud, my wild girl,
pointing them flinty toes,
making the boats rock.
Breathes soft though, she does,
easy, from south-west.

Nicolette Golding

This, Is Where I Hang My Hat

Fence needs painting
As does the garden shed,
Path needs fixing on which we tread,
I read how to do it in the books I've read;
As I laze in a morning in my lady's bed.

Roof leaks slightly from a broken slate,
My ladder's broken, so that has to wait,
The hinge is broken on the garden gate,
As I laze in a morning in my lady's bed

Life goes on at a rapid pace, as
I think of the garden of our ancient place,
Roses climb and cornflowers grow,
London pride gives a lovely show,
There's no other place that I care to go,
As I laze in a morning in my lady's bed.

This 'sceptred isle', this 'blessed plot',
A Shakespeare quote; I muse a lot,
But I have not forgot, the
Fence needs painting, as does the shed,
As I laze in a morning in my lady's bed.

Old in the tooth, past my prime, but
The roots I have are almost sublime,
This blessed plot; it suits me fine
As I walk the path that's often trod,
With brush and paint, past the goldenrod.

Richard Cluroe

Romance Of Standing Stones

Beneath the blue of the summer skies,
Among the heather and gorse,
He leant against the hewn stone
Of the granite Lanyon Quoit,
And in a haze of vision
Shadowy figures drew near,
Crossing the wild heathland
Carrying a leaf-strewn bier.

The Quoit was covered by an earth mound
Formed from the rising ground,
The procession moving slowly
Through the green bracken and fern,
And the bier was laid to rest
At the portal open to the moor,
With a Celtic lament of voice and harp
Appraising the fallen warrior.

And wandering along and upwards,
Climbing the winding way,
He followed on to the summit,
To the immense Chun Castle fort
Protected by ditch and fos,
With inner walls of storing bays,
Steps leading down to the well,
And a gateway with guarded ways.

Beyond the hilltop an even plain
Was dotted with crellas and fires,
Where venison on beds of flaming fern
Cooked in steaming blackened stones,
With bread baked on heated gredles,
Ground from ears of stubbled corn,
While the slopes were dotted with herds of beef
And flocks of sheep with curling horn.

Wandering among the settlement
Of huts with granite walls,
And roof covers of poles and reed
Stored with hung smoked fish or fowl,
With dogs racing by, giving tongue,
Hunting the windswept moor,
As pursuing hunters sought their prey
Of wolf and savage boar.

Following over wild heath
Through vale and rugged terrain,
Where the crellas of Carn Euny
Sheltered against the cairn,
To the standing stones of Boscawen Un,
The circle of longstones to ancestors gone,
Where descendants stood at dawn
And vowed to the rising sun.

And onwards to Rosemoddress
To dreaming in the heather,
Where mystic music filled the air,
With lissom dancers weaving garlands,
He reached out to the maidens,
Hands touching, lips smiling, entwining,
Flower buds woven in their hair,
Fleet of foot, dancing and turning.

With the cool rays of the early morn,
The haunting melody fading away,
His raised hand still reaching out
Towards their gliding image
Touched only the rough-hewn cold granite
And he found himself alone,
For the first light of the breaking dawn
Turned each one to standing stone.

Esme Francis

The Touch Of Home

Green, still and soft is the scene of my dreams,
Where waking sleep takes me on mornings like these.
A wish for an intimate place that I feel,
With comfortable bridges to heartfelt ideal.

Barely disturbed by light hands of a man,
The tilling enough for the food of the land,
Green for the work and the toil given well,
The sound is of bees, and the air's thick and still.

The scent is mown grass and nectar, hot skin,
The summer surrounds the land that I'm in.
Revelling in the countryside of my birth,
Different to anywhere else on the Earth.

My home is light-touched but explored and adored,
Each scene linked to touches of friends, laughs, all stored.
Each tree holds a story with its scent on the air.
Alone, I still feel the caresses and care.

Jordan Holmes

She

Like the sea she thunders; becalms, beguiling,
Moods and movement changing with the crying of the gulls;
Soft waves caress, possess, soul overwhelming,
Pursed lips hiss, angrily pounding rage upon the shore.
Sand advances, retreats; clumsily scattering;
Grass tufts beckon with fingers of swaying sighs.
All is lost, flattened; constrained meek submission,
Obedience forced on reckless passers-by:
Skies of grey pearls lower; threaten, engulf you,
Awaiting the sunshine of her enigmatic smile.

Angela Gloker

The Major Oak

Deep inside the Sherwood studio,
The photo cells of the green canopy
Capture the characters' actions below.
Creating a unique historical album.

John is practising his surly signature.
Henry is learning to light a big fire.
Richard is crusading in the Middle East.
Charles is contemplating giving up the chase.
Robin is training his benefit officers.
Mompesson is plagued by worried villagers.
Green is solving his problems using logs.
Booth is establishing his charitable soldiers.

Boot is getting hooked on drugs.
Raleigh is producing sustainable transport.
Bendigo is swapping gloves for the cloth.
Byron is being revolting about Greece.
Lawrence is chasing Lady Chatterley.
Sillitoe is waking up on Sunday morning.
Torvill and Dean are waving a golden cape
Whilst all around clothes are laced.

Age has granted fame and immortality
To the official camera of the county.
Supported by bandages and wooden tripods,
It still develops the annual images.

The negatives stored in concentric rings.
Their secrets safely locked away in its trunk.

John Harper

The Village In The Valley

It is just a little village
In the rural heart of Kent
A pretty little village
Filled with apple blossom scent
The orchards are a picture
In their springtime pink and white
The honeybees among the trees
Are such a welcome sight.

I watch the kingfisher by the brook
His diving skills amazing
I climb the stile and cross the field
Where sheep are quietly grazing
I love the wildflower meadow
Bluebell wood and little streams
I hear the skylark singing -
But only in my dreams.

How I'd love to stroll once more
Along the leafy lane
And hear the church bells echo
Through the valley once again
It always looked enchanting
In rain, or shine or snow
That little Kentish village
I left so long ago.

Sheelah Collier-Ringer

Poem For Britain

Upright in longitude
the map twists and juts,
furthest the Cornish nose pushed west.
Salted peninsulas of Wales,
ragged Scottish shore,
white cliffs elbowing the channel.

Heathery moors, peaks and fells
breast Atlantic winds.
Showers feed the painted fields
of this green land.

A quilt of time embraces cut stone
of castle, church and cottage,
saga of sward and sword.
Agile minds invented
limited kings, limited companies,
technologies of every byway.
Unheralded work and sweat compiled
a history of peaceful labour.

The people, a recipe
of mingled blood and wandering genes,
Celtic and Saxon.
For everyone and the Bard
the dexterous babble of English,
cherry-picker of the world's words.
The universal language.

Knitted and secure
our little, lucky country.
It belongs to us, you and me.
To us. All of us.

Eric Morgan

Flowers Of The Wilderness

Our last wilderness is the loveliest place
Where peace and solitude mark the hours.
Here are whispering streams and windswept fells
With the birdsong at dawn and the glow of wildflowers.

The silver-pink grasses, the blushing wild rose
By riverbank or beneath the trees.
Each flower has chosen its own special place
Petals turned towards the sun, heads a-dance in the breeze.

All the colours of the spectrum
Daisies bob and poppies sway.
The Pyrenean lily, curled and gold
Breathes a scent to take my breath away.

Examine closely one small flower,
So delicate, detailed, perfect, pure.
No human hand could reproduce
Such a masterpiece in miniature.

Magic names of magic flowers,
Columbine, heartsease, alkanet,
Too many to recall by name,
But far too lovely to forget.

Mere words can never justice do.
Mere mortals barely understand.
When we stop and gaze, enchanted at
This wild and unspoilt, beauteous land.

The Slaggyford Poet

Along The Laughton Road

Laughton country village lies,
Along the Lewis road,
Pretty gardens can be spied.
Little cottages make fine abode.

The church tower rises above the trees,
To Heaven, it shows the way.
Along the tree-lined route one sees,
Farms, cattle and sheep at play.

Dark alders frame the lazy river,
Insects drone among tall stems and leaves
Of yellow rocket flowers, that quiver
Gently, in the summer breeze.

Land beyond rise in patterned fold,
To greet the distant tree-topped hills.
Fields of corn reflecting gold,
Amongst the hedgerow deeply filled.

Unspoilt, countryside, warmed by the sun.
Laced with quiet twisting lane
And footpaths, leading one by one,
Through covered wood, and open plain.

Watered by river, and trickling stream
Rippling by, cool and long.
Creating a land, lush and green,
Concealing life, birds and song.

The river meanders on and on,
And feeds the copious lake,
Filled with birds from home and beyond,
Here summer homes they make.

Oh to be here in the summer's sheen,
Warm and lingering days.
To reflect upon this beautiful scene,
And of Laughton's country ways.

Rita Pedrick

Swindon

Busy, thriving, country surround
Town in a valley, hill look down
In railway workshops steam engine born
Where main workforce earned their corn
Railway work from us torn
A town once stressed, now reborn
Gardens, parks, we have a lot
At fall of season, the colours hot

Many shops, a football ground
Man-made pits, entertainment found
Bathing, fishing, small boats a band
Even a bun to eat in hand
Entertainment for the whole day
Artificial sand beach, where children play
Swings, roundabouts, or slide
On small train take a ride

Our town gardens such a thrill
When church bells ring, your memory fill
In carpets of flowers friends meet
Hear a jazz band, Sunday's treat
Walk hand in hand, a picnic take
Under trees take a break
Goldfish swim in water lily pond
Birds in aviary sing sweet song

Large lake, green land
Fruit and candy from a van
Play football, row a boat
Take a swim, use a float
Sandpit, roundabout or swing
A happy day for all bring
Cup of tea, a sticky bun
Great entertainment, have some fun

On River Thames, take boat ride
Got the water, but no tide
Land a fish, biggest that lived
Kiss of life to fish give
Quaint old village, on Thames ledged
Lovely old church on water's edge
Spend a day, look around
Many a walk can be found

Wiltshire has a beauty rare
Mother Nature placed it there
Lucky Swindon has centre place
Makes pleasant home for human race
Best of both worlds, water, land
Each day your entertainment planned
Swindon town a place to share
Welcome all, see you there.

Pearl Powell

Songbird

Blackbird standing on the wall, sending out his morning call.
Beneath – the rustling bamboo plays, tender, sweet hypnotic rays.

Beyond the wall, blown spume waves, form frothy figures on the beach,
Swirling, writhing, out of reach.

Grey, misty dawn breaking. Seagulls crying, swoop and sway,
Time to start a fresh new day.

Further afield, mallow, meadowsweet and haystacks dry,
Under a cloudless cobalt sky.

Streams babble by, full of stars, like skies at night,
Nature is an awesome sight.
Mellow day and all that's bright, gently drifts into the night.

Blackbird standing on the wall, yellow beak quivering,
Sounding out his evening call, whilst sea mist rolls in damp and shivering.

Carole McKee

Hurrah For London

The city of London is extremely busy;
Whenever I go shopping I get awfully dizzy.
If I stand in a queue my place gets taken,
I've often felt downtrodden, abused and shaken.

If I speak out someone may grumble of course,
And ignore my plight and begin to curse.
With family and friends I have lots of fun;
But when they're all gone I'm . . . on . . . my . . . own . . .

If I visit the doctors to ease my pain,
The depth of confusion is so hard to explain,
So I whisper a prayer as I sit with the throng;
Hoping that nothing is seriously wrong.

The house I live in is over sixty years old;
To be quite honest it is dreary and cold.
I have a huge garden, a dog and a cat;
I carefully feed them so they will never get fat.

With TV and radio, laptop and mobile
I can close my front door and relax for a while.
No threat from my neighbours, no fuss and no fights,
Though things could get out of hand throughout the night.

And with public transport running day and night,
Never mind the shoving and occasional fights.
I'm happy and free, I'm in a good mood,
I go home; feed my pets and enjoy my junk food.

I'm excited about living here in this town,
In spite of the rush hour things do settle down.
Some are on the go twenty-four seven
And some act as if they are in heaven

Welcome to London, this is where I live,
It is very cosmopolitan, hectic and expensive,
Look around you, listen to the sounds,
The place is buzzing, there's music all around.

Hurrah for London is all I can say.
Now I must leave you and be on my way.
I don't know about you, I don't know your mind,
But if you reside in London then we're two of a kind.

Beverly Gooden-Wilson

Free

The true land of the free,
must be saved,
God bless our Queen,
and fight to the grave,

but our ethnic diversity,
we must also protect,
triumph over adversity,
but use our intellect,

it's our sense of nationality,
for which our forefathers died,
but use your rationality,
while keeping your pride,

nationalism, can too be extreme,
our tolerance makes Britain great,
we need to follow the British dream,
and not bow down to hate.

Keith Ellinson

Great Britain

Great Britain
home to sixty million
a country you can thrive in
if you put the time in.

Education, equal rights, a gateway to salvation.

English breakfast
bangers and mash
toad in the hole
Sunday roast

and fish and chips you'll find hard to resist.

A nation living in harmony
churches next to mosques
loving thy neighbour
as in holy books

cultures and faiths, mutual trust.

A land of green, breath-taking scenes,
rivers and brooks, ponds and streams,
woods and mountains, autumn leaves,
parks and gardens pathways to dreams.

There's nowhere else I'd rather be.

Flowers blooming, blossom trees,
an oasis to relax with ease,
rabbits, peacocks, swans and ducklings,
children squealing, laughing, running.

Precious memories just keep on coming.

Remnants of castles from time gone by
stately homes that bring history alive
museums and galleries, treasures and gems,
caves full of wonder to capture your heart.

It really is a work of art.

Farms and zoos, safari parks,
guided tours of city's charms,
wherever you go you'll grow to adore
the more you see the more you'll fall.

The Great British Isle has it all.

Maria Shaw

From A Grateful Soul

Golden sandy beaches,
Rolling hills and vales,
Sky and sea embracing-blue,
Wonderful, welcoming Wales.

It's a little rain, or maybe more
That makes the grasses grow
To clothe the fields in emerald-green
And make the rivers flow.

A beautiful land, well beloved
In a world that has grown so small
And we can't forget our men that died,
The boys that rose to the call.

This could have become a foreign land
Instead of this home that we adore
So can't we all cherish this country,
Never again to send our people to war.

Cariad

The Medway Estuary – Kent

The light of the sky
The green of the grass
And a glimpse of Heaven above
Is what I see

The river is high and
The birds are feeding
The gulls are in a frenzy
They all want to be first

Gillingham Country Park
Playing cricket with our grandchildren
With the best of catches ever
There could be

As I look around and see
The delight on their faces
Which is where I want to be
Ice cream – maybe chips for tea

The memories are great for me

Chatham Historical Dock Yard
A stone's throw away
So famous through history
A great day out for the family

Rochester is the place to visit
People come from afar to see
With a castle so grand
The best in the land
Just to think it's for you and me

The cathedral it stands
By the castle so grand
Poised as ever – in beauty
We sit by the river
With a sandwich or two

As the people pass by
Enjoying the view
And the little boats
Glide by with a wave for you

O what wonders to see
And just be
Part of where you live

The flowers in May
That blossom in June
In this lovely county of Kent
The church bells chime
To tell you the time
To come and pray

In your beautiful church – today
Where time stands still
So you can gather yourself
And thank God for everything
That there is

As the light fades away
In the Medway
In our home we stay
My husband and me
With our family.

Val Backs

An Ode To My People – My Town

I love the lovely language,
I hear strolling up and down;
The B offs here, the F offs there,
Which echo around our town.
It makes me feel so homey,
For I'm Anglo-Saxon too,
And it's grand to hear the old tongue,
Given such prominence by you.

Edward Lyon

Eastbourne – A Great Place To Live

Between the sea and the downs
Lies an Edwardian town
It has theatres, a pier and a
Promenade of carpet gardens.
Walk from Fisherman's Green to
Holywell where you can drink
From an everlasting spring.

Summertime there's the kidzsafe
Beach, lifeguards, beach huts.
Dotto trains from Holywell
To Harbour Reach, the Falling Sands
Where at low tide, rock pools to explore.
There's music at the bandstand,
And fireworks at the Redoubt.

In winter the days are short
And crisp, the sun a muted ball
In a grey misty sky. The sea
Has ever-changing colours from
Indigo to light green.
Everything glistens with frost.
We walk along the promenade
Feeling happy and serene.

Elizabeth Jenks

Lake District

(In Memory Of Diesel Dog)

By Castle Rock in Craggly Dale
The striving weeping willows wail
And aspen leaf all a-quiver
Glimmer by the shimmering river.
Grazing rock with agate sheen
Stands against a chancel screen
As buttressed walls rip through the green
To greet a rain-flecked lowering sky
Bossed by racing clouds on high.
Riven rocks and grasping fern
Divided by the bounding tarn
Cling to granite rock divine
Unmoved by Man and hands of time.
Surging springs and rippling rills
Decked out in native rustic frills
Abound among the land-locked hills
Carpeted by daffodils.
Once forged, an ice-age iron band
Covering this ancient land
Threw up giants yet to stand
Amid the boulders' ancient scree
Whose words of praise
Would rise to thee,
And gain them immortality.
Their names resound in English lore
Remembered for evermore
Evolved a tapestry through time
Designed by majesty sublime.

Saxon Knight

Why I Love Hayes Kent

We need to land, they all agreed, as fuel was getting low
Within their spacecraft they could see the dials begin to glow
The trip from Mars had started well, though, unsure of location,
They'd missed the chance to stop at Pluto and find a petrol station
'Just look down there,' cried Captain Zog, 'I see a place to land.'
'It looks like Earth,' the others replied, 'there's hills and sea and sand.'
They checked their maps and decided that a landing would ensue,
Preparing to dock, they checked the wheels, and Zog went to the loo.
'But where shall we land?' asked Martian Zug. 'It's such a difficult choice.'
They ummed and ahhed and scratched their heads, then came a small wee
voice
'I think I have the answer here, we should let destiny rule our fate
There's only one country that thinks it's so good that it's got the prefix Great.'
They all huddled round and studied the maps, landing gear ready to drop
'There's a good place,' shrieked Commander Zig, 'that is where we can stop.
I can see a Shell station and plenty of shops and a green bit where we could
descend
It looks really flat and there's plenty of room to cushion our spacecraft's big
end.'
And that is the reason why Hayes has a hill, and a common with dips and a
pond
It's a great place to live with Zog, Zug and Zig with whom we've created a
bond.

Graham Hayden

A Place I Once Knew Well

The village started with a greyhound track
Large houses stood off the road, way back
Surrounding Fairfield House, the Squires Hall
Sporting gothic pillars and castellated walls
Landed gentry, JP, and a pin-striped banker
Landscape gardener, even a silken barrister

In contrast, across the road, a mere stone's throw
Spencer's Place, small terraced cottages in a row
Struggling poor people but the salt of the Earth
Majority knew no other life been there since birth
The post office for generations run by one family
Now passed to Miss Roberts, 'No Dogs', Emily.

Next to the pub, local hostelry, Hawthorn Inn
Saloon, smoke room and snug harboured sin!
Appeared to be the source of constant tension
No proprietor, stayed to qualify for a pension
Banwell's, the cobbler, boot and shoe repairer
There's more, he was an entertaining raconteur

A farm. Several older villa rented properties
As was the custom, sharing with other parties
Baptist chapel. Rev Richard Jones presided
From the school lane downwards there resided
Accountants, drapers, professionals, to the core
Salesmen, teachers, doctors and general store.

Bill Monington

Autumn Mists In Dunkerton Valley

Autumn's breath dances gracefully with the mists;
they twist and turn, gliding through Dunkerton Valley,
leaving a trail of white satin in their path.
The trees sway, stretch out their limbs,
extending their leaves like fingernails
for the sun's rays to paint,
in lavish luscious golds and reds.
And the stone walls on the winding bridge
are showered in droplets of dew.

A few quaint houses are scattered
across the valley, perched here and there;
gradually showing their presence to the world,
with a gentle glow of light, or flick of the curtains
and the wood burners send trickles of smoke
that encircle the chimneys like a silk scarf.
But the farmer has already stirred,
awoken by the birds and animals' call,
telling him it soon will be morning.

The half-awake commuter arrives,
breaking this scene of perfect serenity;
with his roaring engine and muffled music,
now wishing he didn't have to be elsewhere.
He descends down, down the winding valley,
into the glinting white folds of cloud.
But the City of Bath is an impatient lady,
she taps her watch, as the day is now breaking,
reluctantly the mist lift their curtains,
for her call, the commuter must obey.

Martina Wyatt

Manchester Town Hall

Come walk with me the cobbled square
And follow Albert's frozen stare
Towards the corporate castle where
Committee men and women share
Cathedral quiet and ancient air.

For this is Alfred's towering grace,
It haunts you with its sense of place,
The ghosts of clerks who scratch and pace
As pale as gaslight on the face,
Worn wood, smooth stone, their only trace.

Come walk with me the spiral tread
Up to the rooms where hang the dead
In portraits that the years have bled
To hear like them the minutes read
And time hang heavy on the head.

For this is Alfred's winning pile,
In Spinkwell stone, Italian tile,
In municipal gothic style,
From parapet to pillared aisle
A monument to spatial guile.

David Hulme

Summer City Streets

Hard-baked city streets, concrete pavement overheats
Scorched from repeated summer temperature retention
Weathered by infinite pounding beats of multifarious feet
Solar shimmer haze of urban troop convection dancers

Reflective cool swing doors, air con bargain hunter stores
Display windows dressed with boutique fashion temptations
Mannequin busts haute couture, new season must-have gear
Latest release album, new blockbusters, all techno TVs

Ice cream, sun skin care, check out aisles of pre-packed fare
Fresh percolated frothy coffee bar, pungent aroma
Subway littered art graffiti, tunnel vision dark and dingy
Pelican crossing beeps, matchstick men fluorescent flashing

Rainbow patchwork canopy awn, city grime market stalls worn
Musty books, trinkets, fresh fruit and vegetables
Multi-filled rolls and chips, tea in plastic bendy brimmed cups
Assorted sticky kaleidoscope sweets in misshapen box rows

Strategic placed bench seats, weary shoppers there retreat
Laden logo plastic shopping bags filled to bulging
Office admin pause from working, paper trail tasks aborting
Break out lunch escape, sun and sustenance sandwich munching

City hall clock towers, cathedral spire to heaven scours
Landmark steeples steeped in history, skyline defining
Narrow cobbled backstreets, ancient castle walls feats
Riverside green, canary yellow, traditional hot mustard

Folks mingle and mardle, clammy toes in fountain paddle
A resilient musician strums for loose change busking
Waiting, congregating, park and ride passengers queuing
'Welcome to Norwich, a fine city – premier division'.

Shirley Clayden

Summertime Show

The smoky blue sea peppers kisses along the sand
Fluffy white clouds part with the rising sun
Seaweed laced between smooth pebbles
A gull's chirp signals the day has begun

On goes the suncream
Off come the tops
Chip bars serving
Among the sweet shops

Ice cream licked
Souvenirs bought
Children exhausted
Sun has been caught

Pack up the bucket
Pack up the spade
Home for tea
And some time in the shade

Down calms the shore
Peace is restored
Tide rolls gently back in
Then out once more

The sun has gone leaving a shadowy world
Sand glistens golden in gentle moon glow
Water laps lazily to and fro
Tomorrow will resume the summertime show.

Lyndsey Frost

Mine!

After a dark grey showery day in May
When the sky becomes blue and the sun shines through
Fluffy white clouds slowly drifting along
My heart is filled with a special song
For, looking up, I think all that I see is mine!

When I look out on my own little patch
With the lawn so green and flower hues so lush
And see blackbirds' beaks full of worms or grubs
And sparrows and wrens in and out of the bay-leaf maternity bush
And bees buzzing around in their purposeful way
And hear robin's loud song in my garden each day
I smile with great pleasure for they all are mine!

When I'm by a river flowing through pastures green
Or in a town or city where its use by Man is seen,
I remember finding a bubbling spring
Whose outpouring waters became a little clear stream
Rapidly tumbling down the grassy hillside
Before plunging into a short water slide;
Then on gentler terrain in the valley below
It found a pond which it rippled through
And the pond, half hidden, safe, yet 'alive'
Is a natural haven for up-land wildlife.
Now when I think of that bubbling spring
I have a secret and the secret is mine!

When I drive along some of our country roads
Be they bordered by fields and hedges or Derbyshire's stone walls
Crossing cattle grids into National Parks where hill-sheep are wandering
Or on heather clad moors to see wild ponies roaming,
On the chalk Downs or in the Yorkshire Dales
In beautiful Lake District or to Tarr Steps in Devon
Discovering lochs and glens north of Hadrian's Wall
Snowdonia's landscapes or the fens of East Anglia
The charm of the Cotswolds or the bleak aspect of Bodmin
Somerset's Cheddar Gorge or Sherwood Forest near Nottingham
Each English county having its own distinctive identity
With its own built-up areas and its own little villages
Some being famous for their picturesque thatched cottages
And most showing a feeling of rural serenity,

Wherever I am, wherever I go, not far away is a changing view.
It's up to us all to keep it fresh and 'new'
Not littered with rubbish as thoughtless people do
And as I reflect on our country's scenes and times
I marvel at such a heritage and proudly say it's mine!

When I think of my travels around Britain's shore
And in my mind's eye see the great ocean with awe
The Atlantic pounding the cliffs in the west
The sea lapping sandy beaches with a gentle caress
The picturesque harbours along Scotland's east coast
The wild ruggedness of which western isles can boast
The huge rolling waves of surf riders at Rhosneiger in Anglesey
The Isle of Wight waters for the yachting fraternity,
From John O'Groats to Land's End and to the White Cliffs of Dover
The flow of the tide never ceases its momentum.
Whilst children happily build castles in the sand
And many holidaymakers stroll along the Strand,
I breathe in the exhilarating fresh air
Look out to the horizon where the sea meets the sky
To a beyond where such depths of wonders are
And crafts, great and small, their passage do ply,
Though sharing it with others, to me, the seaside is mine!

Yes, I pay my taxes, dues and demands
Contribute to English Heritage, Woods, Wildlife and National Trust Lands,
When there, with pleasure, I make the most of the time,
Forget the expense, for in paying, all Britain is mine!

Agnes Hickling

T'Lancashire Wakes

The great cotton mills of proud Lancashire, chittered and chattered for most of
the year.
Women were deaf with the rush and the roar, backs bent and broken, hands
red and sore.
They worked weary hours far into the night, saved every penny just so they
might
forget all their troubles and try to escape, on a steam train to Blackpool
for t'Lancashire Wake.

They danced through the night at the world famous Tower, gasped with delight
at the sea's mighty power,
hitched their skirts high, tucked 'em into their kecks, ran to the shore on rough
wooden decks.
Rode on a donkey, ate fish and chips, travelled by tram on one of the trips,
sailed in a boat on Stanley Park lake, when they came to Blackpool
for t'Lancashire Wake.

To ride the great wheel they flocked by the score, hearts beating wildly, they
shouted for more.
By the light of the moon, they strolled on the pier, casting shy glances as
t'young lads drew near.
Laughed at the side shows, giggled with glee, then pushed to the front so that
they could see.
Then at day's end, a ride they would take, in a Landau, down t'prom,
for t'Lancashire Wake.

The looms are now silent in proud Lancashire, no work to be had for many a
year.
The mills sad and empty, the workers have gone, the Wakes Weeks forgotten
as history moves on.
The folks who have brass travel further away, and just come to Blackpool for
only the day.
The mile that was golden can no longer be found, and hearts that were golden
are no longer around.

But, still, in its heyday, our Blackpool could make them all want to come
for t'Lancashire Wake.

Christine McCherry

On Fontmell Down

These pastured ridges eat into the sky.
Billowing they ride
to turn and twine
Ying Yang into each other's arms
and curve like a horse's spine.

Pliable downs swirl
as stretched clouds fly,
sweep
foaming with meadowsweet
to wash at our feet
where the gully curls
dropping away beside.

Wind's fingers and trotting sheep
scratch strata runnels deep
in the hill's hide.
Below, lanes, cottages and farms
settle: time's shed debris, stones
left where tide
withdraws.
            By lowered light
delineated, long, long downs emerge,
heave their white bones,
huge hips and thighs, shoulder and elbow
to rise dripping gorse and spurge,
thistles and orchises from the rippled surge
of fields below
and open themselves to night.

Juliet Austin

A Hymn For Scotland

Grant us the lasting bond that builds a nation
In which no one stands alone
Eager to share the burdens of our neighbour
Off'ring shelter to the stranger
Placing the needs and welfare of the many
Above the riches or the profit of the few

We hail this standard of Scotland
Our homeland
Both ancient and new
Let the nation display its merits
As a beacon, a haven
To the peoples of the world in all we do
May we give them cause to value
Caledonia
Homeland Scotland
Alba the true

Show us the wealth of all we have in common
Over skin, or race, or creed
Make us unstinting in our care and welcome
For all those in fear or need
Happy to spread the fruits of our good fortune
With open doors and open arms and open hearts

Teach us humility so we may temper
Over-pride in our achievements
Keeping in mind this land is ours to safeguard
Not as owners but as stewards
Bound by a solemn duty to replenish
For all the future generations of this earth

Give us the strength to turn away from conflict
And to foster understanding
Seeking to bring together warring parties
On a path to co-existence
Planting the seeds of hope on fields of battle
As advocates for dialogue and compromise

Lead us to wisdom in our rule and justice
Finding truth that knows compassion
Putting our faith in reconciliation
Not revenge nor condemnation
Earning a name as fair and open-minded
Forever honest in our dealings with the world.

David Gasking

My Patch

Living in the Lake District
loving its moods and weathers.

Walking the gentle fells
climbing their rocks.

Sailing on Coniston Water
swimming in Tarn Hows.

Riding a horse or
cycling in spectacular scenery.

Joining in shepherd's meets
enjoying country fairs.

Drinking local ale
eating local food.

Seeing the sunrise tip the mountain peak
watching the sunset from Walney beach.

Wandering away but always
returning to my patch.

Lilian Cooksey

My Home

Albeit village or town
city or region
the United in Kingdom
Is where I follow my seasons.
Yet I think of my home
on a broad global scale
on the Great Planet Earth
I would journey life's trails.
Because I do not need tribes
to bring me release
no anthems or boundaries
do I need to find peace.
God's world is my homeland
with a moon for my guide
I am never alone
In this haven I reside.
A big picture so boundless
painted with all-knowing face
so ancient in wisdom
set in awe-striking grace.
Diverse religions and cultures
that I so want to taste
so home sweet home I will roam
timeless and grandly spinning in space.

Hilton James

Where The Heart Is . . .

World-renowned actors tread our boards
Drawing in theatre-goers by the hordes
But it's not their homage to our famous bard
That makes leaving this place impossibly hard

Setting free thoughts to roam the greenway
The landscape, a painting; yours for the day
Isn't the reason why this town of ours
Is like being an astronomer, surrounded by stars

The Elizabethan architecture, Shakespeare's legacy
Which adds to the romance, preserves history
Isn't the magnet that attracts to this town
The unwary visitors who end up rooted down

Floating on the Avon, an oar in each hand
The notes splashing over you from the bandstand
Isn't why people who once loved to roam
Now are compelled to call this place home

The thing that makes Stratford on Avon much more
That keeps the tourists queuing at the door
Is the wonderfully friendly atmosphere here
And in all of the pubs, great British beer.

Karl Turner

Heaven Is Where You Make It

Why on Earth am I here?
There's nowhere else I fear
Explore infinity and disappointed, reverse
Via a parallel Universe

You realise how lucky you are
To be on this planet
So well placed from our Star
Good nature did plan it!

The temperature's just right
With air to breathe
We have day and night
Who would want to leave?

We have water to sup
Distilled as rain
Continually lifted up
To drop down again

Happily I'm here today
Cos there's no other place
Where I could stay
Ideal for the human race

Now where on Earth would I wish to stay?
It's here, where I am today
And what part is that pray?
You should know, the UK!

My coastline is varied, the best they say
Rolling countryside, roam where you may
Something different to see all the while
I live in Dorset, I say with a smile

Seaside resorts, with large sandy bays
A wonderful county in all sorts of ways
Market towns, picturesque villages, historical places
For a holiday folks, it has all the aces

A prevailing south-westerly breeze
Skims across unpolluted seas
The air is fresh and invigorating
Pure, uplifting and so bracing

With easy access to other places
It certainly has all the aces
Fly from Hurn airport or go by ship
Tour by bus or rail, enjoy a trip!

The UK is great
Where you can think as you please
A much admired State
By those overseas.

John C E Potter

An English Summer Night

Stretch out your fingers and catch a dream,
The sway of the flowers, the sound of a stream.
The earth's smell of perfume after the rain,
The birds in the hedgerows, sweet songs their refrain.

Silver edge clouds in a deep purple sky,
Touching the moonlight as stars glide by.
The swish of the ocean, the sound of the sea,
The water like silk, sparkling and free.

The blackness of night, silent and still,
The peace of the heavens, beyond the hill.
No crying of seagulls, no sound in the air,
All nature sleeping, free from care.

The waves gently rolling as they ebb and flow,
The sea calls in whispers, soft and low.
Dawn slowly rising, a dim early light,
The owl hoots goodbye to a cool summer night.

Susie Field

Wild Warwickshire

This county's rolling landscape,
On Precambrian rocks to the north
Red sandstone centrally and
Blue lias clay south-east,
Hosts attractive habitats
For insect, bird and beast.

The southern quarry sites of days gone by
Now provide homes for the rare *small-blue-butterfly.*
Bird populations in decline elsewhere
Enjoy a welcome claw-hold here.
The lakes and rivers in the north
Are favourites for some types
Providing ideal nesting grounds
For lapwings and the snipes.

So if you twitchers wish to glimpse them
Plus the bittern, barn owl, song thrush, or chiffchaff
Then ramble round our rolling fields and hills
And through the broad-leaved woodlands
In this county of *The Bear and Ragged Staff.*

David Brough

Thoughts From Far Away

I live to see another spring,
in England's lush, rolling green.
Where lambs are full of gambolling
in meadows, by bright tumbling streams.

Far in the distance hamlets rise,
to peep a roof above green hedge.
New morning brings a pale sunrise,
sharp glint of gold, on sloe and sedge.

This light that flares, its glow unique,
unseen in any other place.
Will paint a blush on English cheeks
not found in distant, far landscapes.

I gaze upon a patchwork scene,
snugged careless over hill and dale.
Such beauty soothes my heart serene,
held soft by river, hedge and vale.

Miki Byrne

Milford Haven

The sea, the ships and the distant fields,
I see from my conservatory;
There is something moving all day long,
So, much to tell and a great story.

Bard Shakespeare called it 'this Blessed Haven',
And so it has surely proved to be,
For over more than two hundred years,
From whale oil, crude oil, now LNG.

After the whale oil came the fishing,
New docks, high employment and progress
But with it dangers and tragedies -
Then, war years and heroes to impress.

The fishing trade then saw new faces,
From Scotland, from the east and the west;
Marriages and families were blessed,
This still thriving fishing port – the best.

But world war came again and all changed,
Many ships were requisitioned, then -
From both these and the fleet, crews were lost;
Memorials tell stories of brave men.

The fishing survived, but then declined,
When oil refineries and tankers came;
Employment and growth were then restored,
Port and haven were busy again.

This latest change to Natural Gas,
Means safety is much more to the fore;
Two terminals now up and running,
Jobs and security as before.

Still the haven, ships and distant fields
I see from my conservatory;
Although out of sight, a marina,
Where the fish trade brought prosperity.

Tankers, trawlers, launches and tugs, work,
Yachts, dinghies and cruisers for leisure,
Also for both the Irish Ferry;
Watching them all gives us much pleasure.

So you will see from my description,
An active, moving, changing story
Of these vessels, large and small to see -
From my valued conservatory.

Janet Bowen

This Green And Pleasant Land

This green and pleasant land
Where nations walk hand in hand
People drink copious amounts of tea
When things start to get heavy
And consoling themselves
Watching Britain's Got Talent on TV
For those with a touch of class
While away the day with idle chatter
With a drink discussing things
Earl Grey or a drop of wine, just a glass
Stuff to most that does not matter
With just a hint of bias
A nice cucumber sarnie
For when they have high tea
Highlight of the perfect summer
Though to be true and fair
We should all live in harmony
On this island nation we do share.

John Warburton

Steel City

Your team are my religion,
Their grounds are my church,
I feel lost when I leave you,
And I can't wait to see you again.

Many inventions were founded within you,
Many notable people from your glorious city,
Everything you want,
Right there in a jiffy.

When I'm feeling mardy,
Or when I'm dressed in blue,
I'm always so proud,
To say that I'm from you.

So much history unfolds,
When walking through your streets,
So many things to see,
So many things to do,
Such a super city are you.

A small orange factory,
A lit-up quayside,
And under the cover of darkness,
Things don't want to hide.

Where everything is 'proper',
Strong and Northern too,
Flat caps and whippets,
Ash and gennels through and through.

Iconic landmarks surround you,
Many old,
But some new,
But I know you'll always stay true,
To the rustless things you do.

Amy Parkinson

No Place Like Home

I've travelled off to lands afar,
To Egypt where the pyramids are,
In Norway saw the midnight sun
Shining – though the day was done.
Sailed the Danube and the Rhine
In Jerez tasted sherry wine,
In glorious Seychelles – lost for words
Seeing multicoloured birds.

Jerusalem was where we all
Signed our names on the Wailing Wall.
In Athens – a sight one must not miss.
The very famous Acropolis.
And to the 'States' I went to see
Grand Canyon and Yosemite.
Travel beckoned me – ere long
I was off to see Hong Kong.

But what can beat the Yorkshire Dales?
Or valleys green in lovely Wales?
Nottinghamshire where once was seen
Robin Hood in Lincoln green
Lake District with its waters cool
Salmon cavorting in the pool
Devon – where we eat cream teas
Cornwall with its surfing seas.

Oh yes, I'm lucky – travelled far,
But in the world, wherever we are
No matter where we're wont to roam
Believe me – there's no place like home!

Kath Hurley

My Country

I was born in Great Britain just after the war,
Battles and bloodshed I never saw,
Brave soldiers fought to make my country free,
Those soldiers have high respect from me.

Living in Britain gives me peace of mind,
The people here are thoughtful and kind,
People from Britain are far from greedy,
They give to the poor, they give to the needy,
They sponsor, they race, they even go to extremes,
They know how precious life does mean.

We've come through the storms, the floods and bad weather,
And just as always the people pull together,
I'm proud to be British and I'm free to roam,
Britain to me is home sweet home.

Sylvia Ranby

Home After A Long Absence

Once I crossed one or two of London's streets
And talked to homeless people, I then found
I was lost suddenly, who walked around
For four hours, with no cash even for sweets.
I studied the Assyrian depictions
In the British Museum's lion hunts
Then we ate where my father's friend had once
Been 'top dog', in *The Chair* (spared all restrictions!)
In Leeds, a woman from East Germany
Was living with us, giving help for free
My father, grinning, then addressed as 'Kirsten'.
We traded a few phrases, in my Russian,
Then she showed me the way all mouths should crush on
The sound 'München', lips bursting!

Dominic King

Exeter

Exeter is the place to be
Lots of ancient history
Cathedral Square is centuries old
With cobbled streets so we're told.

The land around is lush and green
No ugly landmarks to be seen
The beaches are not far away
One can escape there for the day.

But my deep feelings for this place
Are rooted in my English race
Of generations long gone by
Who lived and worked beneath this sky.

They did not move so very far
Before the advent of the car
The horse and cart was all they knew
Their options were but sadly few.

My circumstances are much broader
But instinct tells me not to wander
From this birthplace of which I'm fond
And have a deep and lasting bond.

Sonia Richards

High Leys In December

I found myself in a glaucoma of mist
thru which a milky sun tried to pierce
the nearness being blurred
like a thumb had rubbed away
                    all form and outline
with distance only measured by sound
falling quite beyond its normal depth

a muslin veil hung over the thaw
cracking under ridges
where water had dulled and frozen
with me stumbling on the hardened clumps
                        across the field
to reach a familiar roadmark
telling me how far forward would be left

carlites were giant owlet's eyes
swooping from out the murky swirl
and what is loved lies farther off
where only the needles of spires
                        can jettison thru
the surest pointers in the chill and damp
that lay between our troubled heart and home.

Brian Stone

Our England – A Heart-Stopping Page

Majestic mountains rise forever
Bathed in coloured shadows of the hours
Castles nestling amidst ancient forests
Fiery creepers reach to the tallest towers

Autumn leaves crackle beneath century's feet
Wind's cry carries echoes of the battle's drum beat
Where elements have ravaged Man and land
And men fought with sword in hand

Wandering hedgerows meander to the sea
As meditational echoes of time are set free
Lush pastures have rested the weariest of men
As they journey on to far-off glens

Swishing of the ladies' gowns, plucking of a lute
Horses' hooves across the cobbles, sounds of a flute
A north wind carries seed heads to crevices high
Where there are ghostly moans and a lost lover's sigh

Every turn and pass is a heart-stopping page
Now earth covers history for all our age
Seeping walls of lichen and fungi
Lost in the haunting gull's cry

There is a misty magic to a purpose of each day
Where life is blessed to grow in every way
For there is a beauty in past and present
With a longing for the new and the morning's scent

Now looming shadows are advancing night's mysteries
As I ponder all that's beauty and such . . . that is history.

Susan Roffey

St John's Church, Cardiff At Christmas

I entered into old St John's Church
where I found solace and tranquillity
away from manic Christmas shoppers.
A vagrant relished the warmth of a wooden pew
as I admired the 15th Century stone pillars,
Christmas tree sparkling in front of me
and as the tower bells began ringing
I imagined the sound of angels singing.

I climbed up the spiral staircase
to the Tea Pot where pictures
of departed workers adorned the walls
as well as photographs of this fine church
taken from so many years ago.
Then I returned to the aisle,
glad to be free from bustling Christmas crowds
as the sun broke through leaden wintry clouds

so that the holy figures on the window lit up
seemingly blessed with a celestial glow.
I wandered as if locked in a dream
to the Prayer Room where I found a poem
written by the famous T S Eliot:
'And prayer is more than an order of words.'
The notes on the Prayer Board made it quite plain
how grateful we should be . . . if free from pain.

Guy Fletcher

This Trump Year

There has been no snow cover in London
This weird, wet and windy winter season
Even on a bitter spring equinox
Until on an early Easter Sunday
In this magical year of mirages.
A white Eastertide instead of Yuletide
To help turn around our upside-down world
With apt favourable, freakish weather!
There is a repeat a fortnight later
With an Olympic flaming fiasco
Over bigger fish eating smaller fish
Hindered not by earthquake lake formation
Even as our predecessors prepare
To host the summer games in this trump year.
Won't the next destination of the torch
Be to where indeed earth-shattering changes
Occur with a bumper autumn harvest?
Reaping the rewards of its odd weather
Despite the ongoing world credit crunch
Uplifting the mind, body and spirit
Whilst counteracting discrimination
Is our Olympic city of London.

Hopes and Fears.

Eunice Ogunkoya

One-Eyed City

Delving deftly into the lyrical kitty
to ponder and pen an affectionate ditty
for the one-eyed city
that never seeks pity
is the abode of the wise and the witty
and even the odd sage with their bunions.
A town blessed with wondrous parks
King Paxton, Queen Arrowe rule
Victoria and Mersey gaze mistfully across the river
to the other side, the Pool.
Prenton Park, the theatre of seems
  seems we're going down
  seems we're going up
  seems that one day we'll win a cup.
Sepia memories of cattle sheds and steam trains
newly weds and lashing rains.
And always the ships ebb and flow
a shipyard, hopefully afloat
ready to build many a boat
as always the ships come and go.
In a world ever so topsy-turvy
good to live in a town so worthy
no mean feats from these keen streets
Birkenhead bred, born but never fed up.
Always end on an up.

Brian Williams

Clapham, London – An Early Sunday Morning

The silence has
the hint of waiting.
For what? It will
not say. Each car
is the vagabond of
noise seen off into
town. The pigeons
peck their way along
the street, the rooks
destroy the garbage
bags. A lonely bus
intrudes, then leaves.
The silence holds
the time at bay
until it climbs
into its ascendancy
reassuring those
drowsy eyes it is
safe to get up.

John Clancy

A Windmill On The Fens

Dawn breaks, great sails in the morning shine bright
slowly great stone wheels rumble the corn to mould
sails turning, the corn is ground, brings flour so white.

Great white sails turning to winds across the fen
facing the wind across the fields strong and bold
the mill turns, as blow you may, no matter when,

Great stone wheels grind the corn from the soil,
flour made for the staff of life it is told
through the long day as wind does blow I toil.

A ship of the land with sails never furled on the mill
men in the mill are sailors filling this ship's hold
when the day is done and all is quiet, my great sail's still.

Night falls, a fluttering of winds, in this stillness sits an owl,
the sentinel to my store of food, its fledglings each other scold
silent in moonlight swoops to the food from nature's bowl.

John Clarke

Grantham Town

Grantham town in a valley lies with hills on every side,
A lofty steeple rising high can be seen from far and wide.
In former days a rural town with a large exquisite church
And an inn with a living beehive sign, river banks with silver birch.
There's a medieval hotel, the 'Angel' it is called
Where kings and queens in centuries past have stayed within its walls.
There's the school where Isaac Newton went – Force of Gravity he found,
Film stars and Prime Minister have lived on Grantham ground.
Through two World Wars, devastating blitz when many lost their lives
The folk of Grantham soldiered on, survived the wars with pride.
The 'Bouncing Bomb' was created here in St Vincent's stately halls.
The River Witham flows through the parks enhanced with waterfalls.
It's a busy industrial town right now with increased population
With supermarkets, skateboard park and sports for recreation.

Enid Hewitt

One Sunday In Spring

Sudbury – a tolling bell
Summoned all to tiny church
I heard this sound across the fields
Walking by the River Stour.

Oh watery world and willow trees
Rushing weirs – so placid now
Silent pools just here and there
No sign of grazing cattle yet.

Bring out your easels and your oils
I think that Gainsborough would be proud
Of this broad canvas in the sun
Mother Nature at her best.

Under endless Suffolk skies
Owners with their canine friends
Stride out on meadows – muddy still
It must have been a flooded scene.

Then back once more to my hotel
(A former mill – complete with wheel)
And to a sleepy Edwardstone
Awash with creamy petal hues.

Steve Glason

Up On The Moors

A walk up on the moor
Feels so very good.
So high up there
I just knew that it would.
The sky so blue.
Sun shining down
Far better than any walk around town.
Walking between the heather
Mother Nature so very close.
The walk was so good.
It's no wonder I boast.
We were not on our own
Plenty people walking about.
Some dressed up in case of rain
But to look up at the blue sky
They dressed up in vain.
It was so lovely, in fact quite warm
It's been so lovely since the crack of dawn.
Days like this make one feel so good
Especially when you're out walking up here.
It was quite tiring
So we stopped to have some tea
But finding somewhere to stop
Was quite beyond me.
Nowhere to be found
So more walking to do
Covering a lot more ground
Back to the car tired out and worn.
So back home to have some tea
And await another dawn.

Keith Rhodes

Through The Gate

I passed through the gate and paused
Looked all around, what would I find?
Or had things changed over the years
I have this memory in my mind.

I looked again, and then I saw
Where I had played so long ago
Faint traces of a hidden path
Where down the hill we used to go.

We'd puff and blow at one o'clocks
Played hide-and-seek amongst the hay
Down to the stream to watch the fish
To see a frog just made our day.

I paused a while to catch my breath
A misty look came into my eyes
When I remembered that special day
When my painted egg won a prize

I made my way down to the stream
Reflecting on the games we played
And how we said we'd all return
Now my memory is starting to fade.

They moved away to pastures new
We kept in touch for many years
Now I come here on my own
As I remember, I hide my tears.

It's time to go, I raise my stick
My helpers are not far away
I slowly go back through the gate
And come to the end of another day.

Barry

I Love Appledore

I've lived in different places
I used to move around
But since I've lived in Appledore
My feet haven't left the ground

I've lived down here for 20 years
It's a beautiful place to be
There's nothing quite like
Living by the sea

I wake up in the morning
Then stroll on down the street
They're all so very friendly
The people that you meet

I take a seat on the bench
To watch the boats go by
There's people there with fishing rods
And seagulls in the sky

Everyone is smiling
Old people holding hands
I look across the water
To see the golden sands

Village life with fishing trips
To whet your appetite
Little kids with crabbing lines
Waiting for a bite

'Hello! How are you?'
Strangers will stop and say
*'Nice to see the sun is out
What a lovely day.'*

Life is easy in Appledore
The sound of singing birds
No traffic jams or beeping horns
It's hard to put into words

If you haven't visited
Why not come and see
For peace and tranquillity
Try Appledore on the quay . . .

Tracey Curtis

Rapture

A quiet cottage in a rural scene,
Trees of plenty and fields green,
Pleasant people all around,
Nature being the primary sound.

A river runs beyond the church,
Birds in melody in the silver birch,
A bridge leading to a footpath,
Flying friends in my bird bath.

Beautiful gardens, flowers in bloom,
The air smelling of sweet perfume,
Bright colours cover the beds
From mustard yellow to crimson reds.

The country spirit runs through me,
There is so much for you to see,
Nature in all its wonderful glory
Can paint a quiet and telling story.

Mark Gittings

The Old Vicarage Grantchester – 23rd April 2006

And have I found the corner yet where the body lies
And the turning calling west to uncrowded empty skies,
By the cramped water. The milled dust creeping still.
Have I turned where you turn to list back on printless toe

Through arches and forlorn hopes – and ages where
Unguarded dust quivers, is gold and brown, drift shivers
Breathes beyond foreign sediments where grey dawns sliver
And grow. Pygmied islands can't keep held what is ours.

Steeped in afternoons and honeyed glow the dewy slanted hours,
And the warm slow murmur of those we used to know
In the undertow; at Grantchester
And all the unquiet hurts are mended still, in Grantchester
Under the mill, under the mill, in Grantchester.

R Toy

The Sussex Downs

I never feel alone when walking on the Sussex Downs
I am hand in hand with nature, nature at her best she comforts me.
It's another world, a world of beauty
I become alive, my senses are responding to all around me,
My troubles left behind in this materialistic world not far away.
I feel in tune with something greater than myself
And give thanks for this beautiful county
It gives me a sense of belonging
I feel my love is shared by many who have passed this way before.

Gladys C'Ailceta

158

The Village

Ethereal bells ring across the green,
A bride in white she stands serene.
Decked with flowers the carthorse waits
Calmly by the wooden gate.
Clouds of petals fill the air,
The carriage awaits the happy pair.

The bowler runs in canvas hat
The clink of ball on linseed bat.
The fielders poised for many a catch
To win the well-fought cricket match.
On China plates the strawberry scones,
Earl Grey tea and ice cream cones.
Midst bees that buzz in purple clover
They sit and chat of maiden overs.

Strains of music fill the air
The flags a-flutter at the fair.
Canvas awnings candy striped
Polished apples red and ripe.
The horses round the field they trot
With plaited mane and ribbon topped.
Children round the maypole dance
The sheep in pens they prod and prance.
A perfect life the English way
The village on a summer's day.

Susie

The Exiled London Welshman

I'm an exiled London Welshman
Nearing retirement age,
But, when the choirs come to London
Duw, I'm the first one by the stage.

The Albert Hall is heaving
On St David's Day
With English as well as Welshmen
Who've come from miles away.

It starts with the tuning of lute and cello
Followed by violins, soft and mellow
Then shufflings and coughing gradually cease
And everywhere there's calm and peace

The conductor bows and takes the dais
And, meets his choir face-to-face
Fathers, brothers and next of kin
Observing the rules of discipline
All brought together in mighty band
All under control of one man's hand.

Some faces young, some faces old
Some faces gentle, some faces bold
Now, when I hear tenors and baritones
All blending in their silvery tones
And, standing like soldiers in a line
I get a shiver down my spine
And when Hen Wlad f'nhadai hits the ceiling
I get this funny choked-up feeling.

And I think with nostalgia of our old chapel seat
Where all the family used, to meet
I recall my mother small and neat
Father mopping his brow with heat
And my brother shifting impatient feet.

Then home to a traditional Sunday supper
Beef, cold potatoes and a good hot cuppa
Then later when the night was long
Mother and Father would sing a song
The favourite was Abide With Me
And usually in the key of 'G'

Then to amuse the smaller kids
My brother would dress up in saucepan lids
With bicycle clips on his baggy pants
He'd proceed to do the floral dance.

And bellowing from the upper storey
Uncle Ben would sing both parts
Of the Miserere from Ill Travatore

Then precisely at the given signal
Mother would get out the old Welsh Hymnal
Then Llef and Cwm Rhondda would fill the air
And we'd feel purified in a world of care
Stronger to meet another day,
Fitter to tread the narrow way.

Everything's different today by jingo
With chapels selling out to bingo
If he could see the pubs all lit
The Reverend Goronwy Roberts would have a fit.

If you had time to listen, I could tell some tales
As an exiled London Welshman I'm returning home to Wales
Yes, I think I'll go for Christmas,
Home to the old, coal fire
I hope the Tabernacle choir will be singing the Messiah.

Audrey

The Alien School

There was once a school of aliens,
Who lived beyond the stars,
They studied distant travel
To a planet beyond Mars

Their project had a focus
Find the perfect destination,
For long journeys in a spaceship
To a Milky Way sensation

The students in an essay
Took great care with each word written,
Told how Earthlings came from East and West
To seek a place called Britain

'Why is UK so attractive?'
Asked the strict galactic teachers,
'We have heard it's full of tea shops,
Rainy days are frequent features

And the inmates dig their gardens,
Eat strong curry with real ale,
Get obsessive over football,
Protest hard to 'save the whale'

Worship heroes, such as Churchill,
Lady Thatcher, husband Dennis,
Watch a ball game, known as cricket,
'Men in White' whilst playing tennis

What on earth makes this place special?
Is it Harrods, M&S?
Or the Queen and her attendants?
BBC or NHS?'

'More than that,' young aliens stated,
'UK is the place to reach,
They have fish and chips and custard,
Dr Who . . . oh and free speech!'

Claire Baldry

Islands

The sea on all sides buffs the coast,
from the camel trail through disused rail-lines,
warping up, like ancient feet and nails, to waves
blue as old copper round the horn of Caithness.
    The seawalls, white, wet yellow by faint sun,
shimmer like a catch of mackerel in a driftnet. This
is how a pacifist speaks about his nation. How
a world-citizen might talk for her country.
    When we were young, on the beach in Whitby,
we spent whole days in search of coloured glass,
we scraped each dark stone off a white stone's back,
seeking the rusty streaks that confirmed it, as Jurassic jet.
    In Perth, we climbed
the deer-hills round Loch Rannoch,
through the close, red pillars of the pines,
fetching rosined cones like treasures from the earth.
    Later, older, alone in North London,
crows cawed cool in Regent's Park. Water is flowing.
The voices of footballers were lost in white air,
and the pound of dry leather on the goalposts.
    The sea on all sides buffs the coast.
This twenty-thousand miles of calm, and surf, and storm.
Islands knurled and roughed, by the prehistoric lathe
of caustic weather and of wave.

B T Joy

East Anglia's Own Farmland

In my life this world I have travelled
And seen many a wondrous thing
And I have heard the different races
Their own countries praises sing

I have climbed many of our world's mountains
And trod burning desert sand
But nowhere have I seen the like
Of East Anglia's own farmland

Green of every different hue
From the hedgerows, fields and tires
Surrounding flaxen fields of corn
Waving in the summer's breeze

The farmer on his combine
A machine that never tries
He daydreams of when once he did that job
Walking behind the mighty shires

Those hot lazy idyllic summer days
As on the lush green grass I would lay
As skylarks soared and sang with joy
And watched the newborn lambs at play

And when the urge became too strong
For me once again to roam
Those fond memories I always carried
Of East Anglia and my home

The folk who hail from East Anglia
Are proud and rightly so
Of their part of this dear England
For no matter where you go

No land is more productive
No worker more keen or skilled
An example to the whole wide world
Of how life can be fulfilled.

Don Woods

Fen

In fields still ploughed by the motioning moon we walk
On planks of tumbled oak back to the end of the world, racing
Dark galloping in before the frost
And the skies that just keep on giving answers
To questions ever hailed
Of rain and ghostly tides and echoes of dead seabirds
Once heard by the crouching moon mad sniggler
On the salt soaked sod of his grassy ditches.
I have fallen in love with this place.
Coasted along its currents and found it to be
The last place. The last, newest, ancient point
Scooped out, re-shaped by pummelled hands and water,
Water, running through holes of mottled light like
We are Gods or something greater.
For He has salt from the tears of mermaids on his seaside snacks.
And he invents a future here from driftwood, foraged steel, cargoes
Of spiralled shells and yet
He wears the weather well.
As scattered islands erupt dank fires
Of mulch and vapour hangs above the pools he stands
And shouts the thrashing winds to *give us what he will.*

Poppy Kleiser

Nomadic Nation

Stretching elegantly
   or inelegantly
John O'Groats
   to Land's End

Poised most nomadically
     amidst a plethora
       of European cities
Irish Sea dividing straits
Hebriddean seaswell
  Snaking down to Cardiff
    in another direction
      entirely

Britain encompasses
  posterity
    replayed
      slow
        motion
          or
        original
          excerpts
          historical
            or
          contemporary
          reflexes
           along
             perimeter
             grid

          Rollerballing
            or
          reverberating
           Reviewed
          in camera shutter
            Red
               Eye
            Shot
               scintillating . . .
            Recollected

            Quite simply

as an
iconographic
panorama
of
Great
Britain

protruding
toecap
above
Atlantic deep
deep
in
the
oceanic
landscape

UK

insistently
stridently
red-blue-white
Union Jack
emblazoned
uniquely
present

Tracy Allott

Leominster

Marches town of Leominster
What is the 'o-in' doin' there?
Why do we speak ye as we do . . .
Few folk seem to have a clue

Superfluous 'o-in' unpronounced
'Lemster' it should be announced
And though it seems to me a 'lemster'
Could be a cross twixt a lemming and a hamster!

Was it Leofric of ancient fame
Gave our town its lovely name?
Or someone of whom we little know
Named us thus to vex us so?

But, 'Lemster' though I'm know in
That there little 'o-in',
Could well be an archaic jest
Whatever – I like Leominster best!

Inkslinger

Bournemouth

Bournemouth in Dorset is a great place to be
A bustling town centre right next to the sea
The picturesque gardens and stream running through
Good shops and good nightclubs, plenty to do
Cinemas and theatres, entertainment galore
Catering for everyone, who could want more?
The Red Arrows' display in the summer, such fun
People enjoying their antics watching how it is done
By the pilots and planes as they soar through the air
Such excitemont, such panache and plenty of flair
In the evening the lights and the fireworks display
Bringing an end to such a wonderful, memorable day
Just come to Bournemouth for a holiday, it's the best place to be.

Anita AJB

England – Our Home

English weather comes as expected to its inhabitants, just as night follows day, and so
With each day at any given moment we can see the whole eclipse of seasons in one.
Summer comes in autumn, winter in spring
Yet the audacity of it all gives us our stiff upper lip, as
We embrace the rare moments of Indian summers.
For our tiny island gives us plenty to discuss
It is our reference of small talk to fill the awkward silences, the
Exchange of words to bridge the gap between two perfect strangers.
Wherever you travel to in our tiny country, traditions follow
Friday night fish and chips, to chips and gravy up North
England surely has a diverse range of characteristics, embedded deep within our roots.
We have unravelled mysteries, we have forged our own history, through
Endless battles, monarchies and parliaments,
Yet what we believe as every day, our very past invites all from across the globe, to
Catch a sight of royalty, to see the architecture of London, unknowingly we have become
The ideal location for global mingling. For our beautiful landscape
So diverse and uplifting has come to
Be admired, for it is our own protector, and it has many a reason
To provide us with an ever-changing yet exquisite backdrop to life.

Emma Maskell

Hull, City Of Culture 2017

This snappy little Yorkshire tyke
Is a city which sprawls along each side
Of the River Hull, then tumbles
Southwards into the restless Humber tide.
A north-east port for northern trade,
It spearheads the road, rail and river flow
To the continent and further,
With ocean ships docking to load and stow.

The city speaks of the old days
Of whaling and fishing in the Arctic seas;
The harsh and dangerous living
Of Hull's fishermen and their families,
And now that living is all lost
Like the lives of so many men and ships.
Linger round dock and marina
And taste the tang of the sea on your lips.

Let the sea winds caress your hair
And watch the lone seagull coasting thermals.
Take a moment to stand and stare;
Absorb the mood of this river city,
Its galleries and theatres;
The Hull Truck where John Godber struts his stuff
With 'Bouncers' and 'Up 'N' Under';
And Alan Plater's plays for TV buffs.

This is where Maureen Lipman lived,
Acting her way to London, full of hope;
Where culture and heritage trails
Merge into a vibrant kaleidoscope.
It's a background for Val Wood's books,
For Larkin's inspired poems of number.
Come and be embraced by its folk,
Come and watch the sun set on the Humber.

Gwendoline Douglas

A Little Girl's Dream

There is a place in the heart of the Fens
Built along the River Nene
Where its Georgian buildings gleam
Little girls dream of becoming
The annual Rose Queen

In July Wisbech awakens
To the heavenly scents
The roses smell of a little girl's dream
Carnations on the table with the
Strawberries and cream

The streets come alive with people
From far and wide to get that
Wisbech Rose Fair vibe

The lorries are gleaming
The children are beaming
One little girl is no longer dreaming
The Queen of the Wisbech people's hearts

The excitement builds as the music starts
She is ready to play her part
For she has been chosen to be this year's
Annual Wisbech Rose Queen.

Alison M Bass-Hunt

Liverpool, Where I Belong

I step down from the train to Liverpool
Wisps of clouds hang from the clay sky;
Dull, cold and wintry.

I breathe chilled freedom and realise
Nothing can break the spirit
Of my metropolis
The city that waits for me.

Since my first kiss its friendly carpets
Has welcomed me to the land of The Beatles
My journey began with a candle in hand

And a thousand ambitions.
My city has built the scaffolding
And responded to my challenge to reign.

This city of culture has overcome the shame
From the days of slave trades
And gave us two great football clubs.

While the three Graces reign
Over the Mersey, its docks had launched
The Titanic, and fostered the Vauxhall cars.

Here, nights vibrate with music
In hundreds of nightclubs
And days thrive with romping
Liverpool One shoppers.

I stroll the highways
And sap the vibrant energy from the city
It holds the cradle of culture
Embracing all races and creed.

It is the queen of cities,
Full of excitement and passion
It thrives in arts and culture
Guiding us to a poetic delusion

When I walk along the streets of Liverpool
I develop wings like the Liver Birds;
And imbibe the spirits of the Phoenix.

Soumyen Maitra

Sunset In The East

A mystery! – How can it be?
The eastern shore with sunset o'er the sea?
Sinks low on mudflat and oft beneath the foam
Where cockle craft and fisher folk can roam.

There lazy Arctic wind shows no regard
Drives blizzard snow, the village pond now hard
Frozen crops lie deep in earthy pall
And cattle huddle, warm, within the barn and stall.

High on a hill the morning mist lies low
Like milk upon the meadows far below
Whilst treetops stand so tall above the frosty scene
And winter sunshine glows pale above the hidden pastures green.

Then early mist at last evaporates
And geese fly out in chevrons cross estates
Find inland fields to feast on sugar beet
Then homeward turn, the western setting sun to meet.

Gerald Bell

Orford Lighthouse

I stand alone upon the shore.
I do not show my light anymore.
Alone and sad I have served my time.
Never again my light to shine.

For years I have served ships and men
Never to do this again -
I don't know what will happen to me.
I will probably fall into the sea.

Why couldn't they move me to a safer place
So I could stand once more
So proud to serve the men of the sea
Does anyone out there care for me?

Brenda Butler

Centuries Of Life At Llandeilo Fawr

Awakening to the choir of dawn birds,
The curtain pulled back discloses
Fields of green dew-sparkling swards,
Jewels of flowers, rich ruby roses,
A haven.

Such a busy history of wars and glory
The scene fulfils a panorama of travel
Through ages of human treads, a story
Of loyalty, enmity, jealousy and to marvel
A raven.

Secure amid three rivers, a resting place
To envy, to entice the footsore to settle.
Fauna aplenty, special white cattle, to grace
Table, enhanced by view; fortifying, the battle
Driven.

Such a gem, although hid, always a magnet
The mystery, ancient transfer of knowledge.
Very early transport from there, here sent:
Roman Road builders, Saints, Austerity pledge;
All given.

Dolaucothi gold for roads so bold, Talyllychau
Abbey a skeleton, as austerity was pushed along,
Royals blossomed Llandeilo as time went by:
Some are awarded, others became less strong;
Each bidden.

The tale of Llandeilo unfolds to show wisdom, bold
Female importance too, multicultural development.
Right from the outset, other countries of the world.
Dinefwr, Dynevor patience, as to learn deportment,
Proven.

As the red sun sets at Dryslwyn Castle, a wave from
Old Dinefwr reminds of Elizabethan beacons, signals
Plenty of thick copses today diminish a hostile storm.
Glowing Towy, Blue Riband quality; singing, light, mellows,

Blinds drawn.

Ceiriosen

A View From River Park On The River Gade Boxmoor, Hemel Hempstead, Hertfordshire

An avenue of horse chestnut trees
Flank a path across the moor,
Be-decking a field of dappled horses
With a foal to mother secure.

A pair of swans nesting on a bank
A fisherman looks on,
While a heron searching for his breakfast
Thin-legged, walks alone.

A kingfisher perching on the lock
With long beak and vibrant hues
Gets ready to pounce upon a fish,
A tasty dish to choose.

A blackbird in a thicket
Keeps popping out for worms,
Nine Canada geese in a flock
Across the water 'honk' in turns.

A tiny wren flits back and forth,
A blue tit tumbles acrobatically,
Whilst a mistle thrush perfects his song
Especially for me.

Resplendent in colours black and red
A narrowboat glides the river bed,
The crew happy, relaxed and tanned
Wave a cheery hand.

These wonderful sights on Box Moor
Are entertaining and thrilling,
Everything is as free as air
It doesn't even cost a shilling!

Florence Scott

May In Eastern England

Spring has come in Malvern,
Trees are green once more.
Some are full of blossom,
It thrills me to the core!
Birds are nesting everywhere,
It's so beautiful to see.
I love it when they come with babies,
Just for you and me!
They bring the babies down my path,
Right up to my kitchen door.
Squirrels also visit – but they come alone,
I give them half an apple
Then they run back home,
To feed some to their babies, who wait on their own,
Then they eat the rest!
Now I'm old I don't go out much
So the garden is my joy.
I love to see the wildlife
In my garden to enjoy
The grass or trees,
Then – to eat the food I give them,
Which I hope will always please!

If it's raining very hard
Or snow is on the ground
I put the food under shelter
And they puzzled – look around!
I make sure they always find it.
Their water dish is close by
So they seem to know and poke about,
It's amazing how they try!
One day I looked through the window
I saw a fox out on the path.
Not a bird in sight of course!
He drank the water I had put
In the birds' 'bird bath'
When he left the birds appeared
To eat what he had left,
Which wasn't much, I realised,
The birds just looked bereft!

So I took them out some more.
They thanked me with a 'song'
As I closed my open door!

Now it's time for butterflies
The colours are a treat
I'm just waiting for the roses to bloom
Then spring will be complete!

Evelyn Eagle

Capital Gains

If you're not in a hurry,
Try Selsdon in Surrey.
A short drive away
We have in our sight
Canary Wharf skyline
With spectacular height.

Foxearth Spur denotes our location
(Easy access – East Croydon station)
To London City,
Business or pleasure -
Short journey equals
Mileage for good measure!

Selsdon is near to countryside,
Woods are close by where foxes can hide;
This is their natural habitat,
Also for owners with more than one cat!

For events in the city
We're close at hand
The best of both worlds
It's really quite grand.

Gareth Davies

Eyes Of My Home

Emerald hands dance in the blistering breeze
Daisies and buttercups being kissed by the honeybees
Spring is giving birth to a natural seize
Opening the golden sun in a gentle ease

The cotton pillows are hanging on to its china white bloom
Fighting with the mighty storm not to loom
I breathe in to taste the morning womb
To fly in fresh euphoria above and over the views

Adventures glitter beyond those rolling hills
I can just see the tops disappear within the misty chills
Melting the silence before the rising shrill
Wishing the traffic wouldn't make such an alarming drill

Blessed with such beauty and tranquillity
Some people seem to forget the romantic visibility
To stop and wander the bird desirability
Before being captured with the dust of vulnerability

The habitat a walk around briskly
Is a small suburb with tender history
With an abbey and submarine factory
Keeping a strong connection for families

A few steps away from the busy responsibilities
Away from the buildings and the town clock ticking endlessly
Are playing fields of our local park and bowling greens identity
Ducks and swans ripple across the crystal pond happily

Diamond grinds whisper one's fantasy
From children running amongst sand and sea
I watch the waves cushion the beach with glee
Hiding from the world feeling free

Venture afar into a woodland scenery
Become camouflaged by the greenery
Watch monarch butterflies flutter leisurely
As the songbirds sing tenderly

Yes this is my home
A little few shops placed tiny away in gloam
Gathering of friendly faces that zoom
Never without a helpful hand or room

I sleep in the silence of the abode
Knowing the hustle is always going to corrode
Life is busy escaping, forgetting what beauty explodes
Within this town
I take pictures and memories
With my eyes of my home.

Emily Ryder

A Place I Love

I'm not a worldwide traveller
But I have been to Hong Kong
The place where I live, I'd like to promote
It won't take very long.

It's a little town in Yorkshire
Well known for its famous moor
That's not its only attraction
I can think of many more.

The woods are covered in bluebells
And heather clothes the moor
The river is good for fishing
And there are shops and cafes galore.

There's putting, bowls and tennis
Swimming baths both inside and out
A monastery and a manor house
Going back to the Romans no doubt.

So come to Ilkley and see for yourself
It really is worthwhile
You will get a Yorkshire welcome
A handshake and a smile.

Constance Dewdney

Ulster And Its Troubles

I've lived in Ulster all my life, and am very proud to be,
A man with Northern Ireland blood, yes that's my history;
Now sad to say for many years, such years they have been tough,
Much innocent blood it has been shed, for many it has been rough.

I don't know what's behind it all, how Man could be so cruel,
To take one's life without a thought, I ask you is it real?
There's wives and children left to mourn, and brothers and sisters too,
There's mums and dads, there's uncles and aunts, there's many and not a few.

As loved ones are left to do their grieving, they're shattered no doubt to the core,
As they mourn the loss of their loved one, well it's something they will never get ore;
Now friends I wish to remind you, that God has said in His word,
That vengeance is Mine and that I will repay, yes such are the words of our Lord.

There are many who bomb and are shooting, causing innocent blood to be shed,
They feel they are justified in their doings, as for a cause they say they are led;
But unless they repent as sinners, and call upon God to forgive,
In Hell they will suffer forever, for their deeds upon Earth they did live.

And so says my poem on 'Our Troubles' – in old Ulster that I love oh so well,
I too am a victim of the gunman, but God spared me I'm glad I can tell;
A bullet was meant to remove me, although injured my life God did spare,
To preach to others about my Saviour, if forgiven in Heaven they share.

So in our wee land with its troubles, and especially not knowing what's ahead,
I'm glad I know Christ as my Saviour, as by His hand I am safely led;
He'll lead me and guide me as promised, as thus and thus saith His word,
Then afterwards receive me to glory, to be at home with my wonderful Lord.

Sydney Ward

A Kentish Orchard

Apple blossom delicately pink and white
Heralding the summer days to come,
Slow dropping down a fragrant carpet on the earth below.
So long ago.
Boughs heavy laden with their rosy fruit
As misty autumn days arrive
And voices of the busy pickers can be heard.
So long ago.
The few remaining trees stand gnarled and twisted,
Their fruits now rot upon the ground,
Nature has claimed this Kentish orchard for her own.
Young saplings now are growing tall
And new oak trees unfurl their fingered leaves,
Brambles and nettles all around their trunks.
No human voices now are heard but everywhere
The air is filled with more melodious sound
As tiny birds pour forth their avian songs.
Wood pigeons coo, jays make their strident call,
And long-legged heron flapping lazily
At dawn leaves tree-top roost
To seek its breakfast in the neighbouring lake.
Deep down within the tangled undergrowth
Small creatures of the wild abound
And dawn brings rabbits out to feed
With wary eye for stalking red-furred fox.
This orchard now is rich in other ways,
Instead of fruit the creatures of the wild abound.

Roma Davies

Hope . . . The Other Option

But then, at the end of the day, when all is said and done,
At the end of the lane, past the BunHausen row,
With their scarecrow hats and Albertine wigs,
Mellow in the low – glow, sun – glow day
Dance on!

Dance past the paddock . . .
Where in the bright of the swaying grassy floor,
A Piebald and a Palomino
Enquire, nodding, of your kindness and your pocket.
Dance on!

Dance past the tents and the small green moving homes,
Squatting in their tidy urban rows . . . where in their topsy-turvy roles,
Fathers turn the spitting pan upon reluctant flame,
And mothers, languid, sip their Pimms . . .
Dance on!

Dance youthful, joyful, over the stile and into the golden corn,
Look at it . . . but see it. Touch it . . . but feel it.
Know it . . . it holds for you a promise,
It is the staff of life.
Dance on!

Dance up the winding, fast up the winding,
Throw up your arms in the clamour of the gull-laden, scent-laden day.
Breathe deep, gasp, choke if you must
Only live it . . . the blueness . . . the wonder.
Dance on!

Dance on . . . You are nearly there . . . Dance on!
You should stop now. Be still. For you are come.
Place your hot hands over your eager eyes.
And pray the gift of sight . . .
Now you may look. Look now
Drink in the sea . . . the Kingdom, the Power and the Glory . . .
For it is there. It is everywhere.
The measure of the smallness of all things.
And you have found it.
At the end of the day . . . At the end of the lane.
Dance on!

Jane Brooks

Untitled

Runcorn has a long history
Dating back to the Roman occupancy
Maybe as early as the fourth century AD
Throughout the Industrial Revolution
Runcorn was at the forefront
During the two wars made an essential contribution

After post war the major employer of labour was ICI
Runcorn had a new market and bus station in the fifties
In Runcorn the population and birth rate was growing high
The population was twenty-six and thirty-five in sixty-one
In the fifties the old transporter bridge had gone

The Mersey Road Bridge was complete in nineteen sixty-one
The most momentous event in Runcorn's history
Happened in nineteen sixty-four under a new town act
Thirty-seven farms and seven thousand five hundred of acres have gone
To make way for housing estates, factories, roads and a shopping city
Runcorn and Widnes became a borough in seventy-four

Over the past thirty years or so
I've seen a lot of things come and go
Not all the changes have been good
We've lost the local pub
It broke the back our of our community
Now our friends, we hardly get to see.

Michael McNulty

Journey Home

There's a regal eagle over the caves
Of the Highland island thundering waves
There's a gale on the rail of the fisherman's smack
Then you're glad when your lad comes sailing back
There's a beach in reach of your holiday travel
Where the sand is grand and the clouds unravel
There's a fair over there on the hamlet green
With the chance of a dance with the May Day Queen
There's a row from the plough from the meadow crest
There's a thrush in a rush to a new made nest
There's a lorry in the quarry with the bending weight
Of the roughest and the toughest of the uncut slate
There's a wait at the gate with lights and bells
There is rain on the train from the Cumberland fells
There's a straining crane and a yellow hat team
And the rise to the skies of a concrete beam
There are rivets in the trivets on the factory floor
And the zing and the sting of the circular saw
There's a cram on the tram on the city street
There's the chatter and the clatter of hurrying feet
There's art too smart on the gallery wall
With a price too nice for almost all
There's a quite bright light in the office suite
There are drones on phones with goals to meet
There's a band on the strand by the sycamore trees
There's a meeting and a greeting of the VIPs
There's a prima ballerina and the swirl of a shawl
And the roars of applause at the curtain call
There's a backing for a sacking at the football match
With a ball too tall for the goalie's catch
There's a school with a rule that you walk don't run
With a head called Fred who isn't any fun
Thero's a new tattoo and a Spanish tan
And a dash of panache in lhe white van man
There's a run for fun by the high smoke stack
Where a gran called Ann is ahead of the pack
There's a one-legged son who is losing his hair
Yet he grins as he spins in his new wheelchair
There's a drifting riff on the base guitar

At a gig too big for the Blue Moon bar
There's fire in the choir at the gospel hall
Where a mother and a brother say yes to the call
There's a queue at the loo at the car boot sale
There are crocks and frocks and a toddler's wail
There's a glad new dad who will praise the Lord
Over newborn Sue in the baby ward
There's a squeal from the wheel on the runway tar
Here's Jack come back from Zanzibar
There is charm in the calm of the college square
There is strolling by the bowling in the evening air
There are rows of crows on castle keep
There's a mound in the ground where heroes sleep
There are herds of nerds who work at night
Selling trash for cash on the eBay site
There is tea on your knee by the garden shed
Where a wren called Ben hops up to be fed.

Norman Herringshaw

My Island Home

Azure blue to turquoise green
The bluest sea you've ever seen
The sky above cloudless but with morning haze
Quiet – heat to come – just sit and gaze
Not a breath of wind – no foliage stirs
The view of small islands slightly blurs.

A gem of an island in the sea
Is where I was born and want to be.
Some come – some go
But often they return and know
Having toured the world but still agree
It's hard to beat 'Sarnia Cherie'.

Jacqueline Bartlett

Sunrise, Sunset

I love to watch the red sunset that covers the hills
The colour of a beautiful sky still gives my greatest thrill
Then the moon and stars appear, nature's fairy lights
They cover the countryside with a soft glow of the night

The forest comes alive, those night creatures are free to roam
Those mother foxes will come from their den-like homes
You can watch the badgers playing under a moon-filled night
There are times that blackness will cover the faint moonlight

Then the countryside will welcome a new day's dawning
Then the sunrise will fill the sky, the start of the morning
The sky is now full of tiny birds flying on their tiny wings
Then the morning choruses, listen to songs they sing

The night hunters are now in their dens, they are now asleep
The fields now filled with cows, horses and some sheep
The hens are in the farmyard, the ducks are swimming upon a lake
The dogs are lying by kitchen door and fox coming thro' a gate.

J F Grainger

Now I'm Sixty-Four

I often think how fortunate I am
To live in such a beauteous countryside.
My place of birth's just nine miles from my door.
When I was eight we moved into a town
But there was lovely country all around.
And now that I have moved to Somerton
I am surrounded by green fields and trees.
In minutes I can walk to scenery
That is most beautiful to look upon
And provides also many lovely views.
Go to the top of Glastonbury Tor
Or by the River Isle at Ilchester
And there is scenery to bless your soul.
I think of all this now I'm sixty-four.

Jillian Mounter

186

River Erme: Devon

Welded to the Erme's tungsten bank
Granite rocks hold grey steely rank;
Chattering waters, soaking, lank
    Sharp stones shaped in their spine.
Those Cornwood Maidens on Stall Moor
Cool vintage girls who've drunk before
This rushing splash and overture,
    Of Earth's organic wine.

Porous peat-stained bronze river bed
Minerals from the Moor are shed,
Copper leaf flowing; russet red
Sourced from where? This energy's head
    Where, finned black trout, onyxed arrow
Flick, twist and bend; darting narrow
    Evading and vulpine.

Reflections of a summer's day
Honeycomb shadows dancing, play
On dimpled, dappled waters sway,
    The world of the piscine.
Tendril lush vines and plump oak tree
Overhang this still shady lea,
Where shattered boulders rest at ease
    Cairns of a river shrine.

Downwards spills roll from misty hills,
To meadow sward and peaceful rill
Once stood a busy watermill
    Now empty and supine.
Aqua gift; Dartmoor's mystery,
Land of tales, ancient history,
Legend, folklore, King's venery;
    A treasury divine.

Ruth Muttlebury

A Perfect Day In The New Forest

Driving slowly on a summer's day
Along the winding roads
The sun is shining brightly
And the countryside explodes

Poppies grow wild in the hedgerows
A pheasant flaunts himself in the field
Families sit by the riverside
Rural life is proudly revealed

Travelling further into the forest
Ponies are roaming with their foals
Children fly kites and play football
And a barbecue exudes its burning coals

Sitting in a quiet spot for a picnic
Surroundings are peaceful and calm
God's countryside at its very best
Pleasant fragrances waft like a soothing balm

Later watching the sun go down
A glowing sunset, a vibrant display
Awash with colour the sky is serene
What an end to a perfect day!

Christina Maggs

Gorleston-On-Sea

With a beach that's long,
and a sparkly sea,
a walk along the prom,
and a nice cup of tea.

The sea becomes a river,
the river becomes The Broads,
boats all of a-shimmer,
people watch with laughter and applause

A theatre that is old,
full of song and dance,
with all the tickets sold,
the audience watches in a trance.

A lifeboat station,
here to save lives,
in a perfect location,
so people can survive.

People in the midday sun,
much to be enjoyed,
all having lots of fun,
and photos taken from a Polaroid.

Joanna Royal

Bromley Town Centre

Planned to create a place to be
Where people can move and feel free.
Pedestrian space in which to walk
Free of traffic, where people can talk.

Enjoying leisure time and life,
Therapy for husband and wife.
Children free to roam in view
Following play and things to do.

Pavement anew, laid with great skill,
Locals and immigrants work with a will.
Showing the value of co-operation
To benefit this corner of our nation.

Gleaming pavings, of quartzite hue
Reflective and sparkling, as they do,
Enhancing business and our leisure
Making shopping more of a pleasure.

Yes, pneumatic drills are not quiet!
But nothing to create a local riot!
New water mains will prevent leaks
When use is at consumer peaks.

But all can see an end to obstruction
As new laid pavings finish construction
With glittering gleam as if they're gold -
As sung in some of the songs of old!

We wait the completion of final phase,
Anticipate a result that will amaze,
Helping people to walk with pleasure
Enjoying each everyday leisure.

Shiny new environment for us
Once over, the work and the fuss,
Underfoot, glows solar lighting
Giving walks a night-time blessing.

Thoughts of recession passing away
With worries of what we must pay.
New environment achieves its aim -
Refreshed town centre receives acclaim!

Jo Allen

Busy, Busy, Busy

Busy, busy, busy, it never used to be.
   Our village is a city now, not like it used to be.
I've seen so many changes here
   Some good, some bad, some shocking,
I used to call on neighbours' homes,
   And help them with their shopping.

When I was young I'd walk along the lanes
   And lush green fields.
Now all I see is roundabouts,
   And concrete cows adorn the fields.

Lots of friends have now moved on
   I can't blame them for that.
Our neighbours have to go to work
   No time to have a chat.
Someday they may just find the time,
   Unless they're in a hurry
But if I go to Milton Keynes,
   I'll be busy, busy, busy.

Jean Windle

O Flower Of Scotland

Silver threads slalom down hillsides
Haunts of larks and Munro baggers
Merging with bubbling brooks
They slide as one, frothing
Over smooth rocks where sheep
Daintily step.
Little bursts of thunder
Signify cataracts ahead
Boiling white water,
Greedily the broad sweep of the river
Embraces and swallows its feeders.
Now the passage to the sea in earnest begins
Through villages, towns and cities
Where its strong and silent flow
Passes barely noticed
Amid the busy human traffic
Drowned in their private griefs
Unless it bursts its banks
To intrude upon those lives
Or becomes the watery grave
Of despairing souls
Surrendering to its cold comfort
At last into the welcoming ocean it washes
with which it shares its salty tales.

Denis Bruce

The Island

Is there a world within our being.
A land within our minds.
A refuge from this madness,
The stress and strain of life.

This land of understanding,
Of love and peace and joy.
Where sun-kissed golden beaches
Meet bright blue cloudless skies.

Where all men live as equals,
No place for hate or war.
Just a peaceful co-existence
On some lush exotic shore.

Let your thoughts do the travelling
Let your mind take control.
There are no walls or boundaries
On your mind, your heart, your soul.

But this place is just illusion,
No more than just a dream.
For this home of peace and refuge
Is just an island of your dreams.

Gwyn Thomas

GB Building Blocks

And a large meteoric lump fell out of nowhere -
The skies were darkened and no sound was heard.
It precipitated into the waters and an atoll
Soon became a recognised land mass
Towards the south there were white cliffs – its western-shaped leg
Full of dashing spume against adverse rocks.
The east was flat extending northwards
With large water inlets and a friable shoreline -
All very fertile for the future.
A spinal column of mountains threw the middle into relief.
The western edge was diverge, with a pregnant bulge
And peppered with legion river mouths and a confetti of islands
As if they had fallen off an overloaded shovel,
With one larger area greened, but mostly in shadow.
Further north the meteoric rock had piled up high
Leaving puddles of water
Leading to the unfriendly sea freeing up two groups
Of scattered island rocks – two communities.
The large mass must be named –
What shall it be called?
Why not Brythonia or even
Great Britain.

Robert Main

Border Village

The WI make pickles and jam,
Alan the butcher
Chops up Welsh lamb,
It's whist on Wednesday,
The library van
Calls every Friday
At Bullocks Bottom.

Bill, Joe and James
Went off to war,
They'd never left
Our village before,
We waved farewell
With kisses galore;
They never came back
To Bullocks Bottom.

Eight hundred years
The church's stones
Welcomed the living
Guarded their bones;
The village tavern
In raucous tones
Keeps poor folk merry
In Bullocks Bottom.

A straggle of gardens
A church, an inn,
A granite memorial
To war-dead kin,
Scandal and gossip
Some lose, some win,
Life shuffles on
At Bullocks Bottom.

Rustic

There Is Nothing To Compare

There is nothing to compare
With summer in the city,
When all the flowers are in bloom
And everything looks pretty.

And London Pride is running high,
That's when London is at her best,
As I walk along her hallowed streets,
My heart swells in my chest.

From St Paul's down to Marble Arch
We have history galore,
The mighty Thames in her majesty
Goes rumbling along the shore,

As she has done for centuries,
And seen the change of ages,
As kings and queens have left their mark
On our history book pages.

And all the famous poets who
In Westminster Abbey lie,
Built by Edward the Confessor
For tourists passing by.

Wherever in the world I roam,
I'm glad that London is my home,
It is a privilege to be
Part of this city's history.

Phoebe Brooks

Location Lincolnshire

To live in Lincolnshire has no equal
I've travelled around and found no sequel,
Bred and born a Lincolnshire yellow belly I feel right regal
You consider me to be a yokel.

There's always lots to see and plenty to do
From historic sites to things quite new,
Wide open spaces and things in lieu
Around every corner appears a fresh view.

Cathedrals and churches and historic sites
Golden sand beaches and plenty to do at night,
Secluded places and opportunity for scrumptious bites
Immaterial whether you're mature, fully grown or no but a mite.

Nature lovers are compensated by what they can see
With huge skies, no light pollution there's no better place to be,
On my bike I can travel, mobility is the key
Using pedal power at the end of the day there is no fee.

Across the county farming is much in evidence
It is the bread basket of the country we can say with confidence,
The food it produces is nothing but excellence
Those who regard us as a backwater is just nonsense.

Years ago the Lincolnshire uprising deemed to put us in our place
With leaders, hung, drawn and quartered we were in disgrace,
We fear neither man nor beast, who would be on our case?
Let us meet our critics and face them face-to-face.

John Waby

Landmark

He was our monitor
It was as though the fates had placed him there
To oversee, in solemn silent care,
The corner where we played.
His was a lofty perch
And we, as children, sought no reason for
His presence on the summit of the arch.
We knew him only as the camel man;
An Arab carved in stone,
The burdened beast recumbent at his side,
They were the graven guardians at the gate
Of a great mill, whose trade and industry supplied
Employment for the mass.
How often we had seen the laden carts
Come groaning down the street
The harnessed Clydesdale gleaming bright with brass;
A folded canvas sheet
Cramp-cushioning the carter in the van.
We stopped our game to let them slowly pass
Beneath the archway to the court beyond
Out of the realms of youth's quick-changing thought
Into another world.

But worlds are merely thresholds leading on
To new doors still unlocked
And vistas yet unseen
Fresh portals open where the old had been
Lending a wider view
And when the jostling juggernaut
Emerged, nor small nor strait,
The stalwart strictures of an old-world gate
Had no place in the new.

Today the arch is gone,
Nor absent shall its once familiar form
Light wistful eyes again.
Cruel the fate which mocked
That staunch survivor of a century
Of bitter strife and storm,
Only to be undone;
Demolished by the quick and easy stroke
Of an uncaring pen.

Walter Blacklaw

My Heritage

And as the sunlight dapples through the trees
Accentuating the shadows on the ground
I know that this is where I belong.
I reach to touch the bluebell carpet
Sheltering 'neath the baby green beech leaves
That autumn come will turn to russet brown

In season the smell of pungent bloom
Heralds cow parsley fringes
And forthcoming new mown hay
Just hear those birds rejoicing.

Oh Buckinghamshire, my county, my roots,
My very life. Your villages and little towns
Quaint accents of your country folk
And overall sheer Englishness.
My home, my heritage. Bury me here when I die.

L Fulker

London!

Listen . . . can you hear the sound of London?
Humming in your ears
On the radio 'Tears For Fears'
Rush hour traffic, toots of a horn
Hurry, worry, in a flurry
Stop for brekkie and a bacon buttie
Catch a red bus, black cab, tube train
Take you to where the action is
Busy crowds going places
Aching feet but smiling faces
Grab a sarnie, have a barnie – for a parking space
 – in yer face!
Football cheers washed down with beers
Bag a bargain, wave a flag
Hustle, bustle, tousle
Shopping trips that take some muscle
Sirens of police cars echo all day
Get out of their way, hey!
Squashed on the train
Caught in the rain, such a pain
Umbrellas and sun hats
Share the same place
Carry both – just in case
Don't worry 'bout a few cool raindrops
London's the place to be!
People watching from behind 'The Times'
Nine to five to stay alive
To pay the rent, dodging double lines
And parking fines
The London look out on the streets
Tap your toes to the crazy beat
Afloat on a boat down the Thames
Wave to the Queen
Pussy cat, pussy cat where have you been?
Pubbing, clubbing, shoulder rubbing on the dating scene
Crumpets with butter or jellied eels
Jogging bottoms or ridiculous heels
Fisticuffs at the night club
Bow tied bouncers at the door

Keep on partying – it's only 04:00!
Snog in the corner or break the law (don't!)
Stay at the Hilton or just B and B
Lavish and luxury behind closed doors
Or step over a tramp – the choice is yours
Ride on the Eye – a spectacle high
Watch jugglers and performers
Or climb The Shard
To be bored in London is very hard
Go to Hyde Park, have a lark
Take off your vest, have a rest
Laze in the sun, frolic and fun
Take the dog for a very long run
Read a book, stop and look
At flowers and trees and birds and bees
Don't crush or rush but lay on the grass
Take a step back and give it some slack
As you sip on your Coke and eat your afternoon snack
Watch the world go by, let out a sigh
Take a deep breath, take stock of the day
Say 'come what may'
Tomorrow you can do it all again
Squabble in the marketplace
Fight for your rights in this rat race
Hot on the heels of the latest fashion
Posing and pouting is the newest passion
One of the liveliest places
Strangers with familiar faces
With so much to see and lots of it free
Selfridges or Harrods is where I want to be
Eating grapes or caviar or beans on toast
Down the pub for a Sunday roast
Go to the theatre and sip on fine wine
Say 'yar' and 'hooraah' and have a good time
London is an amazing place
There's nowhere like it in outer space
From dusk 'til dawn stifle a yawn
Tea and cucumber sandwiches on the lawn
You must go and see a show
Miss Saigon or the Lion King
Champagne or lager

Just get in and swing
Be there, don't be square
Be alive and live the dream
Be seen eating your strawberries and cream
Go where you like, hire a bike
Don't get stuck, try your luck
Wherever you go just remember this
With a kiss, never miss
To discover chaotic bliss . . .
London!

Deborah Chivers

Gravestone Of Love

There is family serenity and peacefulness
In the Sunderland air, around today's gravestone,
As I stand beside my 'late' husband and son,
My mind recalling happy hours we have known.

Midsummer blossoms have now been gathered
From a 'garden of love' at our family home,
And I shall remember dear ones forever,
As beneath England's blue skies I roam.

My 'late' husband and son are now close together
So deep in my memory from days of yore -
One special place in beautiful England
The City of Sunderland – I shall love evermore.

Tyne and Wear country from times long gone by
Means so much in my life today . . .
I am never alone, for I know in my heart
A lantern of love will always be shining my way.

Joyce Hemsley

The Rainhill Trials

The iron-clad monsters
Stood to attention
Spurting so much smoke
That even the most ferocious
Of dragons would have turned and run.

Crowds gathered at a safe distance
They'd heard such tales of these creatures -
That cows dropped dead
In their speedy wake;
But worse much worse

That they swallowed people whole
Through gaps in their sides
And swept them away
To far-off lands
Never to return.

Now here the baying beasts
Waited. Tamed and shackled
Straining to prove that they
Were the best and would
Have that place in history.

The Cyclopede ran well
At first, but faded fast.
While the Novelty sped
Quickly on, amazing watchers
Until its bellows burst.

The mighty Sanspareil
Charged on, until 'wounded'
It retired, weeping water
From a failed pump, then
Perseverance ran out of steam.

The ungainly Rocket stood proud
In victory, the judges satisfied
Opposition defied. It moved forward
Knowing that we would
All follow on these 'right lines'.

Sue Gerrard

Ye Olde Black Lyon

In Epping town, there lived a Beast -
A Siren's Song, a Witches' spell -
That lured the menfolk to a feast
That vanquish'd will and proffered Hell.

It took their heart, their charm, their health.
Their time, it magicked clean away.
It stole their wit, their calm, their wealth.
With bitter stealth, consumed its prey.

At dawn it called in soft, sweet tones,
By noon had promised life and luck,
At sunset, gorged – with savage moans -
And spat men out as midnight struck.

Yet, through it all, the weakened soul,
Deprived of conscience, common sense
And wisdom, would still give his all
Be lost amid a forest dense.

And midst what was perceived as mirth
(But actually a Hell on Earth),
They drank – and gained a gaping girth -
And lost their minds – and all self-worth.

Wives of those weakened souls would be
Impoverished, sans company;
Black Widows for the Beast, you see,
That was fair Epping's hostelry.

But men still swore and took the ale
That wore deep furrows in their brow;
And though their wives might weep and wail,
They'd disregard each Holy Vow.

For still the Beast desired much more;
His heart and soul – his silver, gold;
A Mistress with a Devil's Claw
That took young men and turned them old.

For none could win 'gainst such a force
That sapped their strength, consumed their flame -
Yet thrives today – without remorse,
That Olde Black Lyon of Forest Fame.

Sue Devlin

Britain

The piper twirled a skirl of his pipes
that echoed far and wide
A dancer with magic in his shoes
heard it and then replied
A wandering poet caught the theme
and set it down in prose
From the heart of a singing nation
a song of praise arose.

The Scots and Irish, English and Welsh,
four nations in one land
Called the British all over the world
when they extend their hand
Now why should these islands be so great
I'll tell you what I see
A yarn spun from the finest of threads
cover humanity.

Audrey Parks

Parsons Green

At Parsons Green in summertime
The holidaymakers come.
And in the air across the fair
Sound tambourine and drum.

With a rattle! and a boom! and a boom! Boom! Boom!

The bric-a-brac dealers soon arrive:
Tommy and Billy and Sid.
They spread out their wares on tables and chairs.
(I can see something there for a quid!)

Oh! blessed day to get away
From all the care and worry.
You can smack your lips over fish and chips
Or try the rice and curry.

We smile at each other and wave our hands
In time to the music's beat,
And call out loud among the crowd
To all the friends we meet.

In summertime at Parsons Green
No chance for a nap or a slumber.
On improvised stage there is a rage
Of kiddiewinks doing the rhumba.

The perfume of the bacon butties
And the hot dogs too
Around the fair will greet the mayor
Who hovers into view.

He wears his chain of office here,
The clown his chain of sausage
Around his neck and look – oh! heck!
He takes the mayor a hostage.

In days of summer Parsons Green
An isle of joy it seems.
The sound of laughter long hereafter
Echoes in our dreams.

The day has swiftly come and gone,
The candyfloss to foam.
The clowns on stilts as the afternoon wilts,
Make their way back home.

Sweet Parsons Green at summer's end,
Remember we were there?
But no regret for we are set
To come again next year.

With a rattle! and a boom! and a boom! Boom! Boom!

And a boom!

John Hudson

Nostalgia

I remember the place where I was born as if it were yesterday,
With the donkey stone steps and window sills, and cobblestone streets where
we played.
I remember the spluttering gas lamps too, yellowing in the gloom,
And the coal fires halfway up the chimney, casting shadows round the room.
I remember the long winter's evenings, and the gas light's comforting glow,
And the raindrops on the window sills, in the world of long ago.
And I remember my mum's home-made cooking, especially her jellies and
pies,
And bread being made on the hearthstone, dough just starting to rise.
I can remember the school I went to, with my own little desk and chair,
And the teachers there who taught us, and the nurse who examined our hair.
The coal pits too I remember, slag heaps nearly touching the sky,
And I remember St Anne's Church so well, and its bell with its mournful call,
And the tombstones, silent reminders in the graveyard, that death comes to
us all.
But the dream which most often returns, when fancy takes licence to roam,
Is that of a world which has ended, and a child with his memories of home!

Ed Collins

Sidney Street

I like the street I live in
It's like things ought to be
Some gardens gravelled and some green
And one has a monkey puzzle tree.
The houses are all different
Terrace, detached, a mix –
Some are painted stucco
And some are stone and bricks.
Some people are retired and quiet -
They all lead different lives
Some families with teens – a riot.
They walk their dogs, they wash the car,
Mow the lawn whenever they can
But they'd never use a hosepipe,
If we had a hosepipe ban.
If somebody doing a street collection
Rattles a charity tin
You can bet your bottom euro
They'd all put something in.
The flags were out for England
Hoping for a win
The sunflower seeds and peanuts
Are out for birds to dine.
When you walk along our street
You can feel these honest lives
I like the street I live in
I hope my street survives.

Christine Kennett

Our Homeland

This green and pleasant land of ours
We British still call home
No matter where life takes us
No more we want to roam.

The villages and towns we leave
The modern world, to explore
They call us back so naturally
We don't want anymore

The quietness of village life
Landscapes so serene
The country walks, our great parks
Where very few have been

Our ancient forts and castles
Sentinels on high
Look out o'er fields and woodland
A view we can't deny

Our waterways, viaducts and locks
Heritage from long ago
The palaces, the stately homes
The perfect magic show

This is the homeland of the free
We fought for long ago
Fly the flag Britannia
Let the world know it's our show.

Derrick Harding

That's A Lovely Bit Of Black Country

I spoke about some shoes
'They'm nice, bait they?'
'That's a lovely bit of Black Country,'
A lady said to me.

Detect
In the Black Country dialect
Words of Anglo-Saxon and the Middle Ages
Words in Chaucer's 'Canterbury Tales'
Words in Shakespeare's plays.

In 2014, my uncle George asks,
'How bist? It's stoon code.'
'How are you? It's stone cold'.
He is 82 or 83.

Yes, the Queen's English must be spoken.
But today, so many Black Country children 'speak proper'.
For a dialect to thrive
It must be spoken to be kept alive.

Black Country folk
Of your great dialect be proud!
Spake it, every day.
In Rowley, Halesowen, West Bromwich,
Other towns too,
And the city of Wolverhampton
And pronounce Dudley 'Dudlay'
Or into history our Black Country dialect will disappear
If we don't spake the words
Known to Chaucer and Shakespeare.

Jackie Adams

Forward Poetry
Information

We hope you have enjoyed reading
this book - and that you will continue
to enjoy it in the coming years.

If you like reading and writing poetry
drop us a line, or give us a call, and we'll
send you a free information pack.

Alternatively if you would like to order further copies of this
book or any of our other titles, then please give us a call
or log onto our website at www.forwardpoetry.co.uk

Forward Poetry Information
Remus House
Coltsfoot Drive
Peterborough
PE2 9BF
(01733) 890099